M000158974

An incredible book. As I finished it, I was shocked to have tears streaming down my cheeks as if I'd just lost a dear friend or close family member, even though I'd only met Andy briefly when I was a young actor with The Lost Colony *in the early 1970s. He was much more than just an inspiration to me as an actor—and just as important, for doing what is right as a man and islander—he was an inspiration to millions of people throughout the world and continues to be long after his passing. "You will be remembered, Andy," to borrow the language of* The Lost Colony *bard, Paul Green.*

—*Leon Rippy, actor*

For the first time, here is the real Andy…compassionately explained and understood in all his wild and wonderful complexities…from how he found himself as an artist on our island to then spending much of his life giving back to it and helping preserve its special nature.

—*John Wilson IV, one of Andy's closest friends and a former Manteo mayor*

ANDY GRIFFITH'S
Manteo

⊰⊱ HIS REAL MAYBERRY ⊰⊱

John Railey

THE
History
PRESS

Published by The History Press
Charleston, SC
www.historypress.com

Copyright © 2022 by John Railey
All rights reserved

First published 2022

ISBN 9781540252081

Library of Congress Control Number: 2021952400

Notice: The information in this book is true and complete to the best of our knowledge. It is offered without guarantee on the part of the author or The History Press. The author and The History Press disclaim all liability in connection with the use of this book.

All rights reserved. No part of this book may be reproduced or transmitted in any form whatsoever without prior written permission from the publisher except in the case of brief quotations embodied in critical articles and reviews.

For my parents.
And for Kathleen and Molly, my beach girls.

CONTENTS

AUTHOR'S NOTE

*T*he *Andy Griffith Show* winds like an island honeysuckle vine through this book, as it did through Andy's life and still does through the lives of millions of his fans. I use a popular nickname for the series, "the AG show," in this work. Andy's estate on the North End of Roanoke Island was outside the Manteo corporate limits, but Andy and his fellow North End residents had Manteo mailing addresses and routinely said they were from Manteo. References to Paul Green's *Lost Colony* script are from Andy's years in the play from 1947 through 1953 and do not reflect later revisions.

John Railey
Nags Head, North Carolina
February 2022

ROANOKE ISLAND, NORTH CAROLINA

May 2022

Andy loved Manteo and told me about it all the time. He wanted to leave the minute we wrapped the show for the season and be there as much as he could, to take his shoes off and leave them off for weeks at a time. His eyes would light up any time he started talking about Manteo and the lore of pirates having sailed those waters and all of that. Manteo never left him.
—*Ron Howard, the Hollywood producer and director who played Opie in* The Andy Griffith Show, *in a January 10, 2021 interview with the author*

I will always be indebted to those wonderful people of Dare County because they gave me a place to search for something, and, hopefully, to find it. I will be repaying that for the rest of my life.
—*Andy, speaking in Raleigh, North Carolina, November 19, 1982*

*I*t was dusk, a gray-dog day surrendering to a cool sunset in August 2020. Island friends were taking me out on their wooden sportfishing boat, a thirty-footer with clean lines, a vessel they took Andy out on when he grew too frosty-haired frail to take out his own boat. They knew him well. They told me about enjoying drinks with him on the Roanoke Sound, and we shared drinks as they wove stories about Andy. My friend at the wheel pulled out from his downtown Manteo dock and piloted the boat out of Shallowbag Bay, then cruised slowly north on the Sound, rocking gently by a sandspit where Andy sometimes parked his buddy-laden pontoon boat (he hated to be alone, my friends told me) and fiercely competed in volleyball. We cruised by Andy's last big house peeking through the pines. It's just northwest of the Waterside Theater, the home of *The Lost Colony* outdoor drama, where it all began for Andy in the summer of 1947.

His memories of working in that play were the anchor to which he kept returning. During his six-decade career, he caught countless red-eye flights east from Los Angeles, headed home from the city where he made his living to the island that gave him that living. He'd sip drinks at night high above the lights twinkling on in thousands of heartland homes across the nation where lived his fan legion, first watching his namesake show on prime time

Andy as Sir Walter Raleigh on the cover of a *Lost Colony* program. *Courtesy Outer Banks History Center, State Archives of North Carolina.*

on TV sets with rabbit-ear antennas, then in daily reruns on flat screens. For the last leg of the trip, once he made it big, he'd catch a puddle-jumping small plane to his island, the sight of shimmering water and sand beaches fringed by pines always making his heart sing, the place that eventually became his full-time home.

As my friends told their stories and we rolled across the dream-drifting Sound where Andy spent many of his happiest hours, the island's barefoot legend was coming alive.

What was he really like? This year, 2022, the tenth anniversary of his death, that's the question his fans nationwide continue to ask. We know him as the iconic Sheriff Andy Taylor of his namesake show.

Andy Griffith often said he was not Taylor, nowhere near as good as him, although there were parts of him in that character that, tellingly, bears his first name. In thousands of interviews, he sprinkled clues about his true self, sometimes speaking candidly about his artistic struggles and self-doubt. But he was never clear about who he really was, carefully keeping up his guard.

His closest friends on the island, who knew him best, joined him in the effort, mostly maintaining their silence after his death there on July 3, 2012. But by the summer of 2018, as I worked on another book concerning his island, I sensed something was changing. My sources began pulling out their scrapbooks, volunteering fascinating stories about Andy. I listened,

Andy with Don Knotts and Ron Howard on the set of *The Andy Griffith Show* in the 1960s. *Outer Banks History Center, State Archives of North Carolina.*

spellbound. Andy's island friends were finally ready to talk. They were trusting me with their stories and photos, tales that depicted a man who was in some ways like the TV sheriff and in other ways far different. Some of our talks took place in houses where Andy had partied by the water. His friends would often end their stories with "Well, that was just Andy."

They wanted to set it right, to convey the true nature of this man who was a tangle of contradictions, separating the myth from the reality, as hard as that might be. He was a crack skeet shot and a hard drinker and he was religious in his own way. He loved the gentle, slow-boat pace of the island, where he could pop in at a friend's house and he and his buddy would break out their guitars and tall boy Budweisers, porch-strumming and talking for hours. He was, by turns, good, generous, ornery and thrifty, and he often quietly helped underdogs like he had been. He demanded loyalty but was rarely cynical and often optimistic, retaining a wide-eyed, curious wonder about the world and was sometimes, even into his last years, naïve. He could be humble at times but usually had to be the center of attention. He loved his yellow Labs, naming them for characters from his show and friends, and took any slight against his dogs as an offense against himself.

He was gentle and mercurial, by turns comforting islanders in grief and giving wise guidance, accidentally shooting off a shotgun in his island house and pounding his right hand so hard into a door of his California home he broke it, causing him to appear in his show wearing a cast, his Sheriff Taylor saying that he hurt it in a scuffle with prisoners. Andy was a chronic practical joker, once conning a local friend into eating a horse-manure sandwich disguised as a hamburger. He loved anything with an engine and wheels, a child of the Great Depression buying up cars of that era and cruising around in them, even though some friends said he wasn't that good a driver because he'd be looking all around, trying to take it all in. He fancied himself a skilled carpenter like his father but cut his hands up on home projects. He jokingly tossed around words like *fag* but quietly stood up against religious leaders who preached against gay marriage because they hurt some of Andy's closest friends who are gay.

He could party down with the best of the drinking Outer Bankers, occasionally downing a fifth of liquor in a night in his younger days, and study his Bible like the best of the sober Bankers, sometimes within the same twenty-four-hour period, just another pilgrim on the path. He loved singing gospel songs and one year served as the choir director of Mount Olivet United Methodist Church in Manteo.

At other times, he would dock his pontoon boat at a popular soundside dive bar, the Drafty Tavern, to reload, with his friends, on pizzas and cases of beer, belting out "When the saints go marching out," his twist on the old gospel song, as they lugged their bounty out to his boat.

He made people laugh and country boy charmed them, onscreen and on the island. Sometimes, the lines blurred, his close friends say, and it was hard

Andy (*far left*) when he was director of the Mount Olivet United Methodist Church choir in 1959. His first wife, Barbara, is on the front row, the next-to-last woman on the right. *Photo by Aycock Brown via Outer Banks History Center, State Archives of North Carolina.*

for even them to discern the real Andy. "He was, after all, an actor," one friend said. But when he told them, "I 'ppreciate it," for small and big acts they did for him, they knew he was their real man.

He was a comedic genius, and, at times, a dramatic genius, but he left behind few public written words of his own. What I do know is that he was driven by the power of stories. At the start of his career, when he did his greatest dramatic acting in his film debut as Lonesome Rhodes in 1957's *A Face in the Crowd*, director Elia Kazan forced him to crawl inside the skin of that tortured character and into the darkest parts of Andy himself. "It's a tremendous performance," Ron Howard told me, "but it took a toll on him."

Andy played out all he'd learned on the island about acting: the presence, the resonance, the making his stage marks, but most of all, the insight into the character. Andy played Rhodes as rambunctious, horny, brave, funny, daring, delusional, drunken and uninhibited. Andy's Rhodes was, in many

Roanoke Island. Andy's property is in the upper left of the shot, near the sand spit. *Drew C. Wilson photo.*

ways, a pirate, maybe drawing from island stories Andy had heard about the old-time pirates, as well as the spirit of some of his island friends, with a heavy dose of the Bible-thumping, hellfire preachers he had heard on the radio growing up. Knowing film, Andy would have realized there was no "Rosebud," as in Orson Welles's *Citizen Kane*, to understand Lonesome.

But there is a Rosebud for Andy. It is Roanoke Island, the spot of sand that spawned him as an artist.

When he arrived there in 1947 as a student at the University at North Carolina at Chapel Hill to act in *The Lost Colony*, he was a work in progress, hitchhiking around the island and bumming rides from friends because he lacked a car, having no idea he would become a major comedic actor, and have a serious shot at becoming a major dramatic actor, within the next ten years. He was restless and determined, open to all venues, having tasted what he could do at the Carolina Playmakers, which had, a few decades before, launched another hill genius out of the Old North State, the novelist Thomas Wolfe. Progressive Chapel Hill stretched Andy's mind, but the island took that evolution to the galaxies. It has become conventional wisdom to say his comedic breakthrough was his monologue "What It Was, Was Football," but that 1953 debut in Raleigh came after his real break on the island a year before. And the Raleigh appearance was engineered by one of his best friends from *The Lost Colony*.

The island, especially as Andy encountered it in the late 1940s, when the downtown Manteo streets were paved with oyster shells, is endlessly fascinating, with its ancient live oaks and yaupon trees, a grapevine stretching back hundreds of years, moody Sound waters surrounding and a garden of stone on a quiet side street with eclectic gravestones full of their own stories. But most important to Andy were the human forces of creativity, his fellow actors and the locals who told him their stories. It was, he would later say, an "emotional draw."

He met a people of daring dreams and found a way to tap into their watery ways and make them his own. He listened closely to islanders chatting and interacting and transformed it to comedic art, a style that was all his own. It was, like much of the best comedy, forged in the comedian's own insecurities. Andy was not especially book-wise, but he was rural-road smart and ambitious as all get out, inherently recognizing three fellow actors who could ease his hurt with their art and launch his career, then repeatedly turning to them. He was fired up by the competitive spirit among the cast and by the sexual energy going on all around him, both among his fellow cast members and the locals. He absorbed the islanders' risk-taking spirit, soon rolling the dice on Broadway and in Hollywood.

Some old-time Roanoke Islanders call newcomers "wash-ins." Only rarely do they accept a wash-in as their own. Andy was one of the exceptions, long before he became a star. He was their court jester.

If not for that island that stretched his mind and talent, and the connections he made there, he would never have made it big.

The islanders accepted him and gave him the sense of belonging he had long sought, damaged by being called "white trash" by a fourth-grade female classmate in his hometown, Mount Airy, in the North Caroline foothills. He was an only child with loving and supportive parents, a mother who taught him to love music and a father whom Andy said was a natural comedian in his own right. But Andy had not felt that love from his town. "Once you have s—— on your shoes, you can't shake it off," he said in an unpublished 1982 interview with Outer Banks author David Stick. "You cannot get it off. But when I came here [to the island], I was in the same boat everybody else was....Everybody started from scratch here."

The islanders never stopped loving him and would have done the same if he had remained a small-town high school teacher, working in the play in the summer, like many of his fellow Colony crew members who held full-time jobs in the off-season.

He never forgot it, that boy who never saw the sea before he came to their island, eventually becoming one with the locals. He was there for them in sickness and health in many ways, ranging from securing a jet ride home from Texas for a cancer-stricken beloved to visiting with a sick buddy in Chapel Hill to singing at a friend's wedding. "He did a lot of things nobody ever saw," one longtime island friend, Della Basnight, said.

As the AG show took off, Andy quietly put up the bucks to restart Manteo High School's band. As Sheriff Taylor told his son in the "Opie's Charity" episode of 1960, you have to give back.

Andy poured lessons he'd learned on the island into his show. "If Mayberry is anywhere, it is Manteo," he told Manteo author Angel Ellis Khoury for her 1999 book *Manteo: A Roanoke Island Town*. He also said, "Mayberry is not Mount Airy."

Mount Airy annually draws thousands of visitors to its fine September celebration of the AG show, Mayberry Days, claiming to be the fictional town's inspiration. Geographically, the show, with its foothills and lake references, was loosely set in Andy's hometown, although Manteo, with its old courthouse from which the sheriff worked, anchoring downtown streets surrounded by modest businesses and cozy homes, was close on the town setting. But most important, the overarching theme of supporting flawed friends—and strangers—and rarely judging them, even those on the wrong side of rigid laws, laughter into healing, is straight out of Andy's heart and feel for his island, a vibe he never felt in Mount Airy. In a 1960 episode of the AG show, "Stranger in Town," Sheriff Taylor ends the show with a powerful speech to his fellow Mayberry residents about welcoming a quirky newcomer and not judging him.

As Andy became a star, he broke his carefully constructed privacy to give back in a big way, becoming a powerful voice for Manteo's revitalization and preservation, reeling in the governors who were his friends and the purse strings they controlled. He helped start the Outer Banks Community Foundation, assisting locals facing a wide range of problems. When Andy made his comeback in the 1980s on prime-time TV as *Matlock*, the flawed, funny and winning lawyer, he filmed a segment on the island to bring its inhabitants needed money, a glorious homecoming for him.

Later, to support friends who ran local grocery stores and fight a chain store coming in, Andy spoke out at meetings and did a commercial, free of charge, putting in hours of retakes to get it right, taking the production as seriously as he had his AG shows. He helped in a push to provide the children of Manteo with free internet access for their schoolwork.

In those efforts, Andy was playing out what Sheriff Taylor would have done had he the means.

Among Andy's contemporary artists from North Carolina and Virginia, the actress Ava Gardner—from modest Tarheel roots like his—became a citizen of the world. The novelist William Styron left Virginia and settled in Connecticut to write his groundbreaking *Confessions of Nat Turner* and stayed there. But Andy, while maintaining a California house for most of his career, remained centered at his Roanoke Island

Andy during the filming of "The Hunting Party." *Drew C. Wilson photo.*

home, its people and *The Lost Colony*. He and his first wife bonded in the play before marrying. Years later, he met his third wife through the colony, the one who would be with him until the end.

Summer after summer, night after night, Andy would anchor his boat at the Waterside Theater and pad barefoot up to the backstage, all long-armed and loose-limbed, his hair a stormy mess, cigarette in hand, thrilling young actors and actresses with a few words, encouraging them to go for it by the Sound as he had, slipping off into the moon-cast water before the show started, not wanting to steal their limelight.

He inspired numerous *Lost Colony* hands, including North Carolina native Leon Rippy, who would go on to be a star character actor, most notably in his roles in *The Patriot, Saving Grace* and *Deadwood*.

For the *Lost Colony* crew and longtime Outer Bankers who would see Andy barefootin' around Manteo town, he was the epitome of coolness, hard work paying off, blowing off steam with partying, Hollywood cool come home to see them. Long before Jimmy Buffett, Andy defined the fun-loving island locality way of life. When Buffett performed in Raleigh in 2014, two years after Andy died, he and his band played the theme song from Andy's show, "The Fishin' Hole."

Ernest Hemingway had Key West, then Bimini, then Cuba, restlessly moving on, leaving island homes in his wake. Andy's first love of an island remained his only one: Roanoke, roughly the same size as Manhattan, the island where he soared early on.

Andy backstage at *The Lost Colony*. *Aycock Brown photo, Outer Banks History Center, State Archives of North Carolina.*

He learned resilience from the islanders, shaking off career setbacks and figuring out his next act, again and again. The locals had his back, and he had theirs. Their stories about him are as contradictory as his nature. Some of his closest local friends say he was mean when he was young and grew nicer as he aged. Others say he was nice when he was young and grew grouchy as he aged and dealt with serious health problems. They all love him, now and forever.

Andy was, like many of his fellow islanders and fellow Southern artists—including Hank Williams Sr.; Jerry Lee Lewis; and Johnny Cash, with whom he starred in a TV movie—frayed and forged by the tension between dreams of heaven and nightmares of hell in the Christ-haunted South. Andy first dreamed of being a Moravian minister, then spent most of his career working hard and playing hard before, in the twilight of his life, doing gospel albums and ribald film roles that harkened back to the powerful promise he'd shown as Lonesome Rhodes and gained him a new set of fans, young ones.

He had long since tapered off hard liquor but did not give up the white wine he loved, albeit sparingly, until near the end. Shortly before his death, he raised his hands in prayer and reembraced his faith in a small church near his beloved Roanoke Sound. He was mourned by North Carolina governors, the president and the *New York Times*.

His incredible rise from early childhood poverty drew clichés like "grit and determination," and there was that, but there was nothing clichéd about this American original. He was deadly serious about being funny as all get out in his own way, making big money with it and giving back to his island. It is all true and all real and all Andy.

In his complexities, he was much like many of his fellow islanders: He wanted to be a good man.

NAGS HEAD, SUMMER 1952

THE SHRINE CLUB AT WHALEBONE JUNCTION

You have to remember: We knew him before he was famous.
—Della Basnight, one of Andy's best island friends, August 2020

The wild-eyed, rail-thin foothills boy steps out on the stage. Andy Griffith, sweaty and scared, is making his first real try at comedy. He is twenty-six years old. The room is crowded and hot, electric fans and salt air drifting through the open windows the only relief. It's edging toward midnight on a Saturday. The audience members, sunburned men in suits and loosened ties, their hair slicked back by Brylcreem and their women with bouffant hairdos in flowered dresses tight on their curves, are blowing clouds of smoke from their unfiltered cigarettes. Some are rowdy, gulping drinks poured over ice, some with mixers, some straight, from the fifths they've brought into the private club in brown paper bags. The scent of aftershave and perfume swirls in the air.

Andy's on the ground floor of the two-story frame building at a junction named for a seventy-two-foot whale skeleton hauled off the beach with a Model-T Ford truck during the Great Depression and eventually placed in front of a gas station to lure in tourists.

The bones had sat there in the yellow, briar-spurred sand, bleached white by the sun, until the station burned down and someone carted the bones

Andy made his comedic breakthrough in 1952 in this Nags Head building that now houses a Catholic church. *Photo by Kathleen Railey.*

away, legends making way for new ones. Andy is sober, having just peeled off his Sir Walter Raleigh costume at *The Lost Colony* outdoor pageant across the bridge over the Roanoke Sound, on Roanoke Island, and changed into street clothes, dark pants, an open-collared shirt and black leather shoes, not the bare feet he usually sports when not working.

Well, almost sober. Andy might have taken a couple of quick shots on the short ride to the Shrine Club with his pageant friend Ainslie Pryor, Andy riding shotgun in Ainslie's station wagon. Among the pageant and island friends Andy has made, he is known for enjoying and, usually, holding his liquor. He has a contagious gap-toothed grin and zest but is serious about his work, obsessed with getting it right before he goes on stage. As Ainslie drove Andy up the Causeway, the car windows would have been down, the damp salt air pouring in, the dimming lights of the island over the Sound water in the rearview mirror, the bright lights of Nags Head ahead, the limitless ocean beyond.

Back at his college, the University of North Carolina at Chapel Hill, after first pursuing a career as a Moravian minister, Andy decided to major in music, then started acting in the Carolina Playmakers, which funneled actors and crew to *The Lost Colony.*

In the pageant, Andy has honed his dramatic acting. He has been a cutup since grade school, and now he's flirting, at least subconsciously, with the idea of becoming a professional comedian or, at least, a comedic actor. He'd always been a listener, a deceptively careful one. Andy has what the novelist James Jones, the author of *From Here to Eternity*, once called "this f—— ear" about the gift of loving conversations overheard and transforming them into beguiling dialogue. From the time he'd caught the ferry over to the hard-living, hard-loving Roanoke Island, Andy has been enraptured, listening closely to the stories the islanders tell in their Old English brogue and the humor that comes with it, especially those of one of his landlords in downtown Manteo, Alpheus "Alph" Drinkwater, with his corny jokes. ("Need to borrow a wheelbarrow, you say? Where you taking your girl tonight?")

The unintended humor is even better, as in the Manteo storeowner who never has whatever item you asked for, saying, "Aw, I had that before the war" or asking the *customer*, "Did we used to carry that?" Andy boiled down the storeowner's response to this: "Whatever you asked for, he ain't got."

Andy, fascinated by such conversations, has begun to transform them into art. He merges those stories with ones he'd heard up in Mount Airy, hundreds of miles west in the foothills of the Blue Ridge Mountains, where he'd grown up the only child of factory worker Carl Lee Griffith and Geneva Nunn Griffith. Being called "white trash" as a child cut him deep. "He came down here wounded, and he got more wounded, at first," one of Andy's island friends would remember.

Alpheus Drinkwater, one of Andy's landlords in downtown Manteo. *Photo by Aycock Brown via the Outer Banks History Center, State Archives of North Carolina.*

Andy started in 1947 in a bit part, an Elizabethan soldier, and played that role the following season as well. That second season had been frustrating. He was working in the pageant with two of his best friends from college, R.G. "Bob" Armstrong and Barbara Edwards. Bob played colonist John Borden to Barbara's Eleanor Dare. They were stars, with their characters all but falling in bed together toward the end of the play. Andy was dating Barbara, the daughter of a school superintendent from Troy, North Carolina, and, by some accounts, Bob had dated her as well, back at Carolina. That, coupled with their play status above Andy's, hurt him. As Bob and Barbara swooned to each other on stage, Andy must have been grimacing backstage. His competitive nature was ignited.

By his third season, 1949, Andy had worked his way up to the top male role in the play, that of Sir Walter. That summer, he married Barbara in the Little Chapel adjacent to the theater grounds. She was a beautiful brunette from North Carolina's Piedmont. Andy was healing and growing as an artist.

He and Barbara moved to Goldsboro, North Carolina, a few hours inland, where Andy taught music and was assistant drama coach at the local high school, then moved to Chapel Hill to chance it all on an across-the-state entertainment routine. They continued to return to work at the pageant each summer. At live-stage venues after *The Lost Colony*, Andy tried out comedy routines. It had been a long hit-and-miss process.

In the weeks before he took the stage at the Shrine Club that summer night in 1952, Andy had been working toward new routines with Ainslie and Bob. Bob, a former steel mill worker, football player and World War II vet from Alabama nine years older than Andy, is like Andy in that he is earthy and wild, but unlike Andy, book smart and a natural writer. Ainslie, a Memphis native five years older than Andy, is like what Andy might want to be, urbane and sophisticated. Ainslie had studied drama at a Memphis college, served in the Merchant Marine in World War II and was the director of the Raleigh Little Theater.

He and Andy met in Manteo when Ainslie, who had recently started in the pageant and played Eleanor's father, Governor John White, came over to Andy and Barbara's room one night, drunk, and sat down on the floor and told a joke. Ainslie and Andy started talking and never stopped, feeling simpatico as greenhorn artists trying to harness their talent and dreams. It's the same with Andy and Bob.

The cast had daylight to kill before their nightly performances. They'd drive over to the Nags Head beach, Ainslie and Andy digging their toes in

Left: R.G. "Bob" Armstrong playing John Borden in *The Lost Colony* in the late 1940s. *Aycock Brown photo via the Outer Banks History Center, State Archives of North Carolina.*

Right: Andy and Barbara in *The Lost Colony* in the early 1950s. *Photo by Aycock Brown via Outer Banks History Center, State Archives of North Carolina.*

the sand by Jennette's Pier, watching waves, Ainslie belting out old blues songs as Andy played guitar. Andy wove that work into skits he did at other venues on the beach, but he wanted more.

He had never written a comedic monologue. But he took that up in that summer of 1952, first trying a "To Be or Not to Be" routine, spinning off the scene from Shakespeare's *Hamlet*. Andy didn't think the routine was funny. So, on a hot afternoon in the yard outside their downtown Manteo rooms, Andy told Bob Armstrong to tell him more about *Hamlet*, dwelling on all the characters. Bob obliged. Andy always knows who to go to, and no one can tell him no.

Andy wandered back to his room and began writing a comedic monologue about *Hamlet*, a country boy's take on the play, one taking in the whole work, not just one scene. Perhaps he was influenced by playing Sir Walter, "an Englishman," as he once put it, "with a Southern accent." He loves standing on that stage by the water, realizing that the events that he and his fellow actors are riffing from actually took place on that sand, getting the whole feel of it. Andy had grown into being a dramatic stage presence, absorbing his role, knowing his lines, how to time them, resonate his voice and hit his marks on the stage. The role has become easy for him, maybe giving him time, even on stage, to think about the Hamlet monologue. He can be distracted. Once, he is caught on camera onstage trying to tap down his rowdy hair.

Now Andy stands on the Shrine Club stage. He is under the hot lights, and those over the audience are off for the show. Andy already knows one paradox of live entertainment: Underneath the bright lights, you can't really see the audience out there in their darkness, maybe just the first row or so, numbing your stage fear a bit, but you know they are there and laser-focused on you, and you sure as hell want to hear their laughter. Silence is deadly. He is out there all by himself, an only child who hates to be alone.

Andy, a mic in his right hand, waves his left hand through his untamed brownish-blond hair, high on the top, short on the back and sides by his big ears. His eyes are deep-set and blue, relatively small beneath a heavy brow, intense and twinkling, going hard if he feels slighted. He smiles and begins to weave, in his foothills drawl, his act:

Now I went to see a play right here lately, it was one of them classical plays, and it was wrote by a fella named William Shakespeare that lived over here in the old country a while back. And it's a play called Hamlet. *It was named after this young boy* Hamlet *that appeared in the play and it was pretty good except that they don't speak as good a English as we do. Now let's see,* Hamlet, *he lived in this castle over in the old country with his mama and daddy.*

Andy rolls on with the story of Hamlet's paternal uncle Claudius killing Hamlet's father, then taking up with Hamlet's mother. He tells of the soldiers saying "hark, hark," and how "they said that a lot back then" and how Hamlet "weren't all there."

He pauses, smiling and hoping for laughs. There are a few chuckles, but nothing more. The audience is accustomed to conventional American comedy, short jokes and one-liners, not this strange long model. A few men rise from their seats and hustle their women out. Andy sees that by the exit lights and is glad that he doesn't see his fellow cast members from *The Lost Colony* and island friends among the departed. He has gotten to know some of the bed-jumping islanders, fascinated by their free-loving culture, gay, straight and bisexual, stretching his mind.

He goes on with his routine, tapping into the hills storytelling with which he was raised, blending it with a narrative style he has learned on the island, tying both styles together with humor gleaned from his father and from studying the dialogues of the hill people and the islanders, seeing the world through their eyes and making the ordinary extraordinarily funny, hitting the sweet spot of not talking down to his compatriots but sharing a wink with them at the highbrows. And most of all, the stories from the islanders, coming sweet to his fine ear like lines woven from honeysuckle vines. Andy knows he must become one with his audience members, signaling to them that they are not alone in their struggles running shops and fishing boats. Their backs are against the wall, and so is his. He has tempered his anger at being looked down upon growing up, transforming it to humor that subtly celebrates working folks.

He rolls on. The laughter grows. He is not classically handsome, but something about the intensity of his eyes and his voice, somewhere between tenor and baritone, touches the audience down deep. He is country and invitingly wild and exotic all at once.

Andy realizes he has them hooked, as surely as fish on the lines of his island buddies. He carefully reels the audience in, honing his timing, waving his long arms to make points, reveling in his comedic power.

He lays the hook in hard: "It's a pretty good show, and the moral of it is, if you was to ever kill a fella and marry his wife, I'd be right careful not to tell my stepson."

Finally, the people in the audience cannot stop laughing. They are not laughing at him, like people did when he was a boy, but with him. He is controlling the laughter.

The audience cheers and cheers. Andy smiles and bows. Taking his first bow as Sir Walter was sweet, but this is something else again.

The audience, and the island, have just given him his start at stardom. What happened to him on that sliver of sand during his *Lost Colony* summers, culminating in that night, was as magic as lightning over the Sound, a cosmic kiss. He will never forget it. He will try to repay the debt.

1

HEADED TOWARD
"THE SAME BOAT"

We who were in The Lost Colony *were summer visitors who were to be tolerated.*
—Andy in a 1982 interview with Outer Banks author David Stick

ROANOKE ISLAND

Summer 1947

Andy lit up an unfiltered cigarette and strolled the Manteo waterfront along Shallowbag Bay Harbor, the Sound just beyond. It was morning but not too early. Andy slept late. He worked nights as an Elizabethan soldier in *The Lost Colony*, a bit part as "the First Soldier," but he was striving for more. He wore heavy steel armor for the role. He'd later joke that he felt like a lightning rod, scared of the frequent bolts over the Sound behind the waterfront theater. He was an understudy for the part of Sir Walter.

He was twenty-one, wild and free for the first time in his life, an only child far away from his loving but overprotective mother. He was sometimes barechested on the island, wearing a beat-up straw hat and worn khaki shorts.

And most important to the birth of the legend of Andy of Manteo, he'd started going barefoot. Like many legends, the barefoot part is rooted in the commonplace, the hilariously commonplace. You can see Andy's eyes twinkling as he told the story years later: "I'd come here with athlete's foot, a bad case of athlete's foot. Nothing seemed to help and I took my shoes off and it went right away....I went barefoot down here ever since."

(Going barefoot had long been a norm for the islanders. One of Andy's good island friends, Saint Basnight, said going barefoot eased his own foot troubles, and Andy got the idea from him. At Saint's funeral, his son, Saint Jr., asked Andy why he wasn't barefoot, Angel Ellis Khoury writes in *Manteo: A Roanoke Island Town*. Andy replied: "A little respect, Saint, a little respect.")

World War II had been just offshore a few years ago, "Torpedo Junction," German U-boats sinking U.S. naval ships and their allies, sailors maimed and dying in oil fires flaming on the sea surface. Andy, a music major at the University of North Carolina at Chapel Hill, might have been in the war but for a back problem.

Locals were coming in by boat to do business, some to shop, others to sell their shrimp, fish, oysters and crabs, still others to go to the old brick courthouse to tackle travails of life, charges ranging from fighting to moonshining. The courthouse was a 1904 brick building with white columns, anchoring downtown Manteo. Just over a decade earlier, *Lost Colony* playwright Paul Green, islanders and congressmen had huddled in that courthouse as they sketched out plans for their play in advance of the 1937 premiere.

Andy carefully listened to locals' conversations, the humor both intended and unintended, the workings of small-town life. He loved to study people. He knew the islanders were as wary of outsiders as his hill folk were.

"Now in those days, there were true natives down here, that is, most of the people who lived here were natives," Andy would later tell David Stick. "There were a few people that had moved here from other places, but most of the people were natives. And mountain people...do not accept you right away. They're very standoffish and very clannish. And the islanders—I say 'islanders' because I was more familiar with the island than any other part of it down here—were that way."

But there was something different on the island. "In Mount Airy, no matter how much singing I did or how much what I was still white trash," he would remember. "A girl called me white trash once, and I never got over that....But when I came here, I was in the same boat everybody else was.... Everybody [the colony actors] started from scratch here. You didn't have that background that you had wherever you were from."

He kept walking and listening to the islanders chat. He absorbed all, the hot salt air carrying the smell of gas from the pretty old boats of faded paint on wood rocking and creaking in their slips in the oil-slick water by splintery docks. There was the horniness of the locals and the mourning doves off in the pines with their broken-hearted coos, all of it overpowering his senses. He didn't write it down—that wasn't his nature—but he filed it all away in his brain.

At Carolina, in the cool old town of Chapel Hill, where he lived in Room 17 of the Steele dorm, then in Room 33, he'd been evolving, writing a few letters home in which he addressed his parents as "Dear Folks" and "Dear Mother and Father," signing off with "Yours, Andy." In one letter, he wrote, "Chapel Hill is really one huge park, but we who live here are apt to take it for granted." The school, the nation's oldest state university, had just a few thousand students. Dr. Frank Porter Graham was the beloved school president. He was a giant among the state's progressives, standing up for government help for underdogs of all stripes. A government program had helped Andy with tuition because of his back problem, caused by falling off a rope swing as a child.

Despite the tone set by its president, the campus was in many ways still Old South. Rich boys and girls joined fraternities and sororities. Andy felt he was looked down on as a factory worker's son.

He weighed his intention to become a Moravian minister against his love of secular music. At one point, he went to see a Moravian bishop in Winston-Salem, near his hometown, asking him if he could major in music and still go ahead with his ministerial studies. "He said no," Andy would later recall. "I went back, and I prayed over it and worried about it and finally I went and told the bishop that I was going to leave the ministerial studies and major in music. And he said, I'll never forget it, he said, 'You cannot serve God by singing in musical comedy.'"

Andy chose the music major. And he began to dabble in acting, "foolin' around," as he put it, with his college's venerable Carolina Playmakers. He found a sense of belonging with the artistic set on campus.

In 1946, he heard about a chance to be in *The Lost Colony*. "Oh God, and I didn't have idea where Roanoke Island was, what it was, what *The Lost Colony* was, nothing!" he remembered. "But I did read the play, and I thought, 'Well, that's not too bad.' So I tried out for Sir Walter Raleigh. And I was awarded the part of a colonist for twenty-five dollars a week."

He turned it down, opting to stay home and work with his father at a Mount Airy furniture factory because he could make more money there to pay his tuition. But the work was boring as hell. In his free time, Andy read the few plays available at his local public library.

Back at Carolina, he was offered the First Soldier role in *The Lost Colony* for the same twenty-five a week. He jumped at it. "I remember being very jealous of Gene McLain," Andy would later say. "He lived in the same dormitory I did, and he was gonna play Simon Fernando and get something like forty-five. But he and I made a pact that we were going to live together because you could get a room for three dollars apiece as opposed to five for a single."

In the summer of 1947 on the island, Andy was flying high. Just weeks before, Andy had caught a ride down to Roanoke Island to work at the Colony. His heart must have sung when he caught the ferry from Manns Harbor, the island growing ever larger as the ferry drew closer, the green pines rimming the beaches of yellow sand, small Sound waves lapping at driftwood. Decades later, John Denver would sing about coming home to a place he'd never been before. That's what happened to Andy.

The island, about ten miles long and three miles wide, is bounded on the west by the Croatan Sound, on the east by the Roanoke Sound, on the north by the Albemarle Sound and on the south by the Pamlico Sound. Near the center of the island is Manteo, the Dare County seat, named for the American Indian who welcomed the colonists before they were lost. On the south end of the island is Wanchese, a commercial fishing bedrock named for Manteo's fellow Croatan Indian Wanchese, who had a healthy distrust of the English.

Andy was absorbing it all: the daring, the gregariousness, the joking, the rebelliousness, the fun of the sexually charged island, the crazy conception of stagecraft, uninhibited on its best days. The island became Andy's training ground, his dreamscape. The island was his muse, his source for love and belonging and creativity, encouraging him to be mind-opened.

He began to make friends with the locals, some involved in the play, some not. He started to absorb the island's free spirit. Almost everyone on that spot of sand was, at least, a distant cousin. They joked that they welcomed the few colony outsiders whom they accepted, occasionally marrying into their clans, because it kept them from bearing children with six toes on a single bare foot.

The actors lived together in old navy barracks at the small local airport on the North End of the island, a couple of miles from the theater. "You played these bit parts, but you found yourself down here in this community of interests with other people involved with music and acting....And that's when you, in effect, found yourself," Andy would remember.

They partied around bonfires by the Sound, Andy playing guitar and joining his friends in sharing gossip and stories, dreaming of making it big far beyond the island. Among his early cast friends was wholesome and fun Marjalene Thomas, who'd been in the play since childhood. "We liked Andy a whole lot," she remembered. "He was a good guy."

Andy bonded with the cast as they honed their craft and began to figure out what it meant, or should mean, to be artists. He watched his fellow actors on stage, what they were doing wrong and what they were doing right.

One of Andy's best friends that summer was Bob Armstrong, his buddy from the Carolina Playmakers. He was like Andy, talent-busting-out and even a few inches taller. Bob was playing a star role, that of John Borden, which ignited Andy's competitive nature.

Some days, Andy, Bob and the rest went over to Nags Head and played in the surf. Other days, they explored remote beaches nearby, sometimes competing in impromptu footraces. Andy, with just 150 pounds stretched over his six-foot frame, often won.

The place was laden with wonder and history, the past blurring with the present on sand where the islanders spoke in an Old English brogue: tide was "toide" and ice was "oice." Andy's landlord, Alph Drinkwater of Manteo, had relayed to the world, by telegraph, news of the Wright brothers' first flight, just shy of forty-four years before. In the years since, radio had taken hold, and now, TV was just beginning to take off.

Drinkwater wasn't the only legend still walking the sand.

In the 1930s, with President Franklin Roosevelt's Works Progress Administration money, Albert "Skipper" Bell, a native of England, built the Waterside Theater by the Roanoke Sound, where *The Lost Colony* was staged. The colony had opened just ten years before. The theater was Bell's masterpiece. It was adjacent to Fort Raleigh on National Park Service land, a lush setting that included dense pines and the expansive Elizabethan Gardens with its white and pink begonias sheltered by crepe myrtle trees.

Skipper, who wore a straw fedora, kept an unlit cigar clenched in his teeth. "If he lit a cigar, he didn't do it often," Skipper's son Quentin remembered. His father, tall and with a love of gardening and the outdoors in general, would become a sort of island godfather for Andy. "Andy liked Dad a lot," Quentin said. "Bob Armstrong did too. Dad could fix anything, and that was always impressive."

On July 24 of that summer of 1947, the theater burned almost to the ground. Irene "Renie" Rains, an island native, Carolina Playmaker vet and the costumer for the play, salvaged most of the costumes. Skipper Bell inspired the crew to rebuild the theater. Roanoke Island had already made it through hurricanes, fires, flooding and the Great Depression. It was an isle of survivors.

"Andy and Bob Armstrong said, 'We can rebuild it in six days with the cast helping,'" Quentin Bell remembered.

At a meeting at the Manteo courthouse, more help was gathered as "citizens offered lumber, hardware, tools, trucks, and other supplies, as well as carpentry skills," Angel Ellis Khoury writes in *Manteo: A Roanoke Island Town*. "Working in four-hour shifts, townspeople alongside the crew and cast were able to reopen and rebuild by [the] self-imposed six-day deadline."

Andy looked up to Skipper and Rains.

He would remember that he recognized, for the first time that season, in his words, "a homosexual," and was "hit on," but his focus was on a female singer. "I was trying so desperately to score with a certain lady [but] I didn't score with her nor either one of the fellows," he later joked.

When the season ended, Andy was one of the last to leave their quarters at the airport. In the 1982 interview with David Stick, Andy set the scene: hitchhiking into downtown Manteo and seeing their costumes, deflated of all the character and he and his fellow actors had breathed into them:

> *This life I had found had come to a sudden end. And I walked from the base out the Airport Road to 64 and thumbed into town. That's where I was let off. And I looked down...that main road there and I saw in huge bundles all those costumes out in front of that laundry, and I'm talking about my insides floated down to my feet. And I stuck my thumb in the air, and, after a while, I was in Chapel Hill.*

———◦∞◦———

In the Stick interview, Andy described what happened to him back at Carolina:

> *That year I met a girl named Bobbie* [Barbara] *Edwards. We were singing together in an oratorio, Haydn's The Seasons....I was the bass soloist and she was the soprano soloist, and I started going with her. That year we did the* Mikado, *I played Ko-Ko, she played Yum-Yum. And we were a big hit in that, they held us over for two or three nights....That year, in the spring, she was awarded the role of Eleanor Dare....I was awarded the role of the Second Soldier, and it was tough...because I'm going with a girl and I'm outclassed again.*

Barbara's Eleanor Dare flirts with Bob Armstrong's John Borden at the end of the play, as Andy was stuck in the bit soldier role. "It was difficult," Andy would later say of the 1948 season, adding, perhaps sardonically, of

Andy, as Sir Walter Raleigh, with Queen Elizabeth in the play in the early 1950s. *Photo by Aycock Brown via Outer Banks History Center, State Archives of North Carolina.*

Bob and Barbara, "Bob Armstrong was a wonderful John Borden. Whatever life can be breathed in those two parts in the second act, they did it."

By the 1949 season, Andy had worked his way up to the starring male role, that of Sir Walter. Andy, with his storyteller's sense of history, must have loved Sir Walter's story and that of the colony lost.

Raleigh was constantly calculating—sometimes coolly, sometimes not so much. That writer and man of action was forever fawning over Queen Elizabeth. He explored far and wide and led in establishing the colony on Roanoke Island, but he never set foot in what is now North Carolina, much less on the island. He did, however, orchestrate the 1587 expedition of colonists to the island, following up on two previous, short-lived efforts there. The more than one hundred colonists of all ages included John White, the governor of the colony; his daughter Eleanor; and her husband, Ananias Dare.

With supplies running low, White sailed for England to restock. England was warring with Spain. White didn't return until 1590. His colony had vanished. White and his company had only one big clue to go on: the word

CROATOAN, carved into a post, and CRO, carved into a tree, as most North Carolina schoolchildren, along with many others nationwide, learned. Croatoan, now spelled "Croatan," was the name of Manteo's tribe of the Algonquian. It was also the name of an area of another Outer Banks Island, now called Hatteras.

The colonists may well have gone off with Croatan Indians and assimilated into their tribe, but the mystery has never been definitively solved. Maybe Sir Walter Raleigh could have gotten answers. But by then, Raleigh, whom Queen Elizabeth had knighted in 1585, was falling out of favor with the queen for marrying one of her ladies in waiting without her prior approval. After Elizabeth died in 1603, Raleigh got on the wrong side of King James when his men, searching for El Dorado/the City of Gold in South America, warred with Spaniards, violating the treaty with England. King James ordered Raleigh's head sliced off in 1618.

Andy learned more each night as he took the stage, realizing the resonance of his voice, the raising of an eyebrow and timing, always timing, were everything.

Veteran newspaperman Aycock Brown, the PR man for play, was constantly shooting Andy and his fellow actors. Aycock was always smiling, all camera flashes and smoke from the cigarette dangling from his lips. He was beloved, known for always helping people whenever he could. He was a crane of a man, rail thin and bespectacled with a pencil-thin mustache, often dressed in a Panama hat and a Hawaiian shirt, with two or three big cameras dangling from worn leather straps around his stringy neck. He was also the county tourism director and a frequent photo contributor to the local paper, *Coastland Times*.

Andy learned to know the camera and meet it. He was charismatic and endearing with his piercing eyes, and Aycock's photos caught that. Aycock sent thousands of Outer Banks scenes across the country, pressing buddies to run them in their newspapers, and Andy was in some of them, his first introduction to the nation.

Some of Andy's island friends thought Barbara, just a couple of months younger than Andy, was far more talented than he was and still swear by that. Some say her high notes could even break champagne glasses, like Ella Fitzgerald's, and she had a beautiful stage presence more quietly powerful than Andy's booming style. She was headed for stardom, they thought, but didn't anticipate it for Andy. Andy knew that, and it frustrated him.

But as the season progressed, Skipper Bell encouraged Andy to marry Barbara.

Legendary Outer Banks
photographer Aycock Brown.
*Outer Banks History Center, State
Archives of North Carolina.*

On Monday, August 22, 1949, as the season drew to a close, Andy married her in the Little Chapel adjacent to *The Lost Colony* grounds. Skipper Bell had built the chapel from pines he hand-hewed. For music, Andy and friends borrowed a pump organ from a church on nearby Colington Island. An octet sang Bach chorales. They held their reception, probably with financial help from Barbara's parents, at the Arlington in Nags Head, a sprawling, whitewashed hotel of wood with graceful porches right by the sea and a fine restaurant, a favorite of Andy's.

In the years ahead, Andy and Barbara would reside restlessly in Goldsboro, where Barbara led a church choir and Andy taught music at the local high school, never feeling he was that good at it. They eventually moved to Chapel Hill to devote their time to making it in show business, working their entertainment act at civic clubs statewide, returning each summer to work in *The Lost Colony*, reuniting with Ainslie Pryor and Bob Armstrong.

Those two friends and Barbara would fire-forge Andy's career in the next few years. They would be forever tied, despite death, divorce and careers rising and falling, four souls springing from the postwar years on their dream isle.

2

THE DREAM HOUSE

That place will be ours someday.
—*Andy to Barbara about their future house, early 1950s*

That, according to some locals, is what Andy told Barbara one summer afternoon as they walked north on the beach by the Roanoke Sound in the early 1950s before going to work at Waterside Theater. Andy was talking about a homestead about a mile northwest of the theater. The one-story house on a slight sand hill was not an imposing structure, only about three thousand square feet, but had a smooth stucco finish over concrete blocks, making it strikingly different from the contemporary wooden houses on the island.

Sometime after that walk, when Barbara had a bad cold, a scary thing for a singer, they had visited the house. They knew the owner was a respected doctor from Pennsylvania, Joseph Barach. A local contractor had built the house for the doctor several years before. The front entrance was on U.S. 64, the house hidden by towering pines and lively brush. Andy and Barbara parked by the road, walked up the long driveway and knocked on the door. The doctor received them warmly. "He couldn't practice down here, but he did have a little medicine there in his house and he treated Barbara's throat," Andy later remembered. "And he liked us."

A few weeks later, the doctor and his wife invited Andy and Barbara to dinner at the house. The doctor, Andy would say, "was a nice man. He showed us around, talked about things, talked about the island."

Aerial shot of Andy's original island house. *Courtesy Bea Bell.*

The doctor had given the land a bizarre name for the coast: Mountain Hill Farm. The house itself was a twist on the owner's house in inner-city Pittsburgh. The builder had set the home near the Sound for spectacular views. Except for the two children's rooms and the kitchen, every room overlooked the Sound. The long driveway wound past the house and continued all the way to the edge of the water.

As Andy and Barbara arrived for dinner that night, they would have taken it all in: The twelve-foot ceilings, the large cypress-paneled living room with bookcases, the big brick fireplace with a few ballast rocks embedded, one rock, the doctor could have told them, with a fossil in it. "The living room was dark from the aged wood and looked a bit like what one would expect to find in an English country house," one of Andy's friends remembered. "There was even a small telephone room for private calls." The house had wondrous views of the Sound and, across that sparkling water, over in Nags Head, the yellow sand mountain Jockey's Ridge, rising more than one hundred feet into the sheltering sky. What might have appealed most to Andy is that the house was set on sixty acres of woods with a nice garage for cars. And it had a boat dock.

Andy and Barbara spent their first married seasons living in downtown Manteo, first in attorney Frank Ausband's frame house on what is now Sir

Walter Raleigh Street with his family of three. Andy and Barbara shared a small, low-ceilinged room with hardwood floors and three windows on the second floor, right across a narrow hall from young Steve Ausband's room. In their room, Andy and Barbara must have been dreaming of something like Mountain Hill Farm.

———— ∞∞∞ ————

In the summer of 1952, a Nags Head audience gave Andy his big break, validating the *Hamlet* monologue he'd worked out with Bob Armstrong. "That was his birth as a comedian," said Bert Austin, who saw Andy perform at the Shrine Club and went on to become Dare County sheriff from 1982 to 2002. "He never forgot that."

Andy would later tell David Stick: "There was something lurking inside me. I had an identity, and for the first time in my life, I was a comedian. And I got laughs....Oh I had...what anybody who deals in comedy, those years of embarrassment, from elementary school and into high school, from almost infancy, from before most of us can remember, people laugh at you. And so what people who deal in comedy wind up doing is doing things overtly to make them laugh so you're in control of the situation rather than the situation being in control of you."

Andy and Barbara, having graduated from Carolina, began barnstorming the state, honing a comedy/song-and-dance act, playing every civic club across North Carolina they could, Andy doing comedic acts, playing guitar and singing, Barbara singing.

They knew their conservative audiences and played to them: Barbara, subtly sexy, Andy playing all old-home.

They were road-ragged, rolling red-eyed down thousands of miles of two-lane highways in their beat-down car with Andy's worn guitar in the back seat, their headlights beaming the way past pines and deer dancing in lonely fields fringed by silent cypress swamps.

Along the blacktop, they put precious dimes into payphones to keep in touch with contacts, including Ainslie Pryor, their *Lost Colony* friend who was making inroads in New York and Hollywood for the start of his own acting career. In early 1952, Andy and Barbara rendezvoused in New York with Ainslie. At a key audition, Andy was told he was not going to make it as a singer. "I guess I was somehow grasping at straws, even though I didn't know it," Andy would say. On the train ride back to North Carolina, Ainslie had a little something for Andy: a chance to do his comedy act at Ainslie's Raleigh Little Theater between acts. Andy's second appearance there was during the intermission of *Ten Nights in a Barroom* in May 1953.

Andy chose to perform his "What It Was, Was Football" monologue, a country boy's take on college football games like the ones Andy saw at Carolina. Andy would later say the monologue came to him on the road with Barbara from Chapel Hill to Raleigh and he "never wrote down a word of it." That jibes with his working style.

The play was tanking. Bette Elliot wrote in the *Raleigh Times*: "Two hours of archaic dialogue, missed cues, mysterious hands, dangling sandbags, sailors from the last production, *Mr. Roberts*, transposed scenes, angels from heaven, and such can prove wearing, especially since we saw it all last year and it was better then."

Then came intermission and Andy, heart thumping but ready to roll. Building on the style he'd unleashed at the Shrine Club in Nags Head, he delivered his comedic take on *Romeo and Juliet*, then launched into "What It Was, Was Football":

> *It was back last October, I believe it was...*
>
> *And what I seen was this whole raft of people a-sittin' on these two banks and a-lookin' at one another across this pretty little green cow pasture. Somebody had took and drawed white lines all over it and drove posts in it, and I don't know what all, and I looked down there and I seen five or six convicts a running up and down and a-blowing whistles....About the time I got set down good I looked down there and I seen thirty or forty men come a-runnin' out of one end of a great big outhouse down there and everybody where I was a-settin' got up and hollered....It was that both bunches full of them wanted this funny-lookin' little pumpkin to play with.*
>
> *And I know, friends, that they couldn't eat it because they kicked it the whole evenin' and it never busted....One bunch got it and it made the other bunch just as mad as they could be....I don't know friends, to this day, what it was that they was a doin' down there, but I have studied about it.*
>
> *I think it was that it's some kind of a contest where they see which bunch-full of them men can take that pumpkin and run from one end of that cow pasture to the other without gettin' knocked down or steppin' in somethin'.*

Elliot wrote that Andy's performance was "worth the price of admission alone" and "fabulously funny." Andy, she wrote, "could have held the stage all night and no would have minded."

Ainslie resigned from the Little Theater at the end of that month of May, off to quickly rise in Hollywood, he and Bob Armstrong, also ascending, freely sharing their contacts with Andy.

———

Orville Campbell, a Chapel Hill publisher and record producer, heard about Andy's performance at the Little Theater and soon contracted with him to put out a record of it. That led to Capitol Records buying out Campbell for a deal that would ultimately sell millions of copies. Dick Linke, a veteran New York agent, signed Andy and became his longtime manager. He had an uncanny sense of how to promote Andy's persona. "I remember walking down Broadway with Andy, back in January or February of '54, he would say to everybody, 'I 'ppreciate it,'" Linke said. "When I had heard it about 20 times, I said, 'Hey, do me a favor. Say that all the time. When you autograph pictures, write, 'I 'ppreciate it.' And someday that'll be a household word."

Linke contracted Andy with the prestigious talent agency William Morris.

Soon, Ainslie sent Andy a copy of a bestselling novel, *No Time for Sergeants*, by Duke University grad and World II vet and Georgia native Mac Hyman, about a country-wild military man, Sergeant Will Stockdale. Bob Armstrong also called Andy to tell him about the book, Terry Collins writes in *The Andy Griffith Story*.

Andy loved the book and knew the Stockdale role was meant for him. He called Hyman to press his case. Auditioning with the *Hamlet* monologue that Armstrong had helped him with, Andy landed the part of Stockdale in the 1954 Broadway production of *No Time for Sergeants*, then a 1955 TV production of the play. He met Don Knotts in the Broadway production.

As the Broadway show began a hit, Andy chanced to run into Alph Drinkwater, one of his landlords from *The Lost Colony* days.

"I said, 'Alph, what are you doing up here?'" Andy would remember years later. "He said, 'Oh, I came up here to be on that television show, about the Wright Brothers.' I said, 'Well come on, let me take you to see my play!'

'OK.' So I took him down to a Saturday matinee of *No Time for Sergeants*, put him down in the fourth row, nice seats. And after the show was over, I said, 'Alpheus, how'd you like it?' and he said 'I couldn't tell anything was going on! Every time you said anything they laughed!'"

That's the kind of dialogue Andy filed away for the AG show.

Left: Andy on the set of *No Time for Sergeants* with Ainslie Pryor. *Outer Banks History Center, State Archives of North Carolina.*

Below: Andy kept in touch with beach friends, including John and Elsie May Bell. He invited them to New York to see *No Time for Sergeants* and autographed a playbill for them. *Courtesy Bea Bell.*

Myron McCormick, Andy Griffith and Roddy McDowall in "No Time for Sergeants"

Andy also stayed in contact with Skipper Bell. Bell told Andy that Dr. Barach had died, that his widow had lost interest in Mountain Hill Farm, and encouraged Andy to buy it. Andy, flush with his first show-biz money, could have purchased a cottage on the nearby Nags Head beach, where he often romped. Oceanfront lots could be had for just a few thousand dollars. It was wide-open up the beach, with the raging ocean, wind-whipped sand and the Carolinian Hotel for nightlife. There was also a lot of old money in Nags Head, not the free culture Andy had found on the island. Maybe Andy liked the small-town feel of Manteo, sort of like his foothills hometown but without the rigid class structure.

The cover of the Playbill for *No Time for Sergeants. Courtesy Bea Bell.*

And the island had been Andy's first contact with the Outer Banks. Sometimes, you go with what you first love. Andy, an aficionado of greenery like Skipper Bell, loved the towering loblolly pines that bent but rarely broke in hurricanes, the dogwoods, the live oaks, the yaupons and the crepe myrtles on the northern end of the island, tiny orange trumpet vines growing strong and taut around trees to their tall tops, the sweet smell of honeysuckle vines, the doves cooing from the woods and the deer, squirrels and rabbits at play, all of which he found on the pine straw–carpeted sand of Mountain Hill by the pretty water of the Sound, a peace not found at the beach. In addition, he might have anticipated his growing fame and knew the secluded acreage would give him recluse.

Perhaps most important to him was Mountain Hill's proximity to *The Lost Colony* theater.

On June 21, 1956, Andy bought Mountain Hill Farm from Barach's widow for about $14,000. Andy retained the Mountain Hill name, perhaps a nod to the homeland he had happily left behind. The house came with a garage and a 1953 Ford station wagon, the first of many cars Andy would keep in that garage and on the grounds.

Andy and Barbara had scant time to settle at Mountain Hill.

Andy would later say that R.G. "Bob" Armstrong, who had been in Elia Kazan's 1955 Broadway production of *Cat on a Hot Tin Roof*, was having dinner with Kazan and the director told Bob "of a movie he was going to do about a bum who sang the blues—got on radio, then TV—and became a megalomaniac—a real danger to society. Gagde [Kazan's nickname] asked R.G. if he knew anybody who could play that part. R.G. said 'Andy Griffith can.' And that was the first step toward my playing Lonesome Rhodes [in *A Face in the Crowd*]," Andy told Mal Vincent of the *Virginian-Pilot* newspaper, based in Norfolk.

Two months after closing on their island house, Andy posed with Barbara for a photo for the *Virginian-Pilot* at the Norfolk airport, holding his bound script for *A Face in the Crowd*, headed for Arkansas to begin filming his lead role as Dusty Rhodes, a rookie making his movie debut with a major director. Andy was in a suit, tousle-haired and cockily grinning, a cigarette in his left hand, and Barbara, long-brown-haired beautiful, was beside him in a skirt and sleeveless blouse, trying to smile supportively at him before beginning her long ride back to Manteo alone.

Bob Armstrong took a small role in the film as a TV prompter/operator, a testament to his loyalty to Andy.

The filming would be a mean journey for him.

Before an early scene in which Lonesome Rhodes angrily roars up off his jailhouse cot, Kazan kicked Andy in the back to get his fury up, Andy told an island friend, aggravating his childhood injury. Kazan, a native of Turkey and early leader in the Method School of acting, brash and confident, nineteen years older than Andy and four inches shorter, made clear to him he was the boss, masterfully manipulating Andy's emotions to bring out Lonesome Rhodes. It was graduate school for Andy, challenging the confidence he'd gained in *The Lost Colony* and on Broadway.

After the movie was released in 1957, Andy did an interview with *New York Times* reporter Gilbert Millstein. It's one of the rare interviews in which Andy relaxed his guard, telling Millstein how hard it was to go to his dark side to make the film. He couldn't cut Dusty Rhodes off when he left the set, he said, and sometimes took his brooding self out on Barbara. As filming moved to New York, Andy and Barbara lived in an apartment there. But at the time of the Millstein interview, Andy was alone in the apartment. Millstein wrote:

> *His wife was in Manteo, and he said he missed her. He said he treated her very badly during most of the filming of* A Face in the Crowd. *It was a macabre recital. "I became Lonesome Rhodes," Griffith said somberly. "It was something bigger than I was, and it might have got to control me. It started right here in New York and continued up to the last month of the picture." In order to exact from Griffith the right measure of arrogance, self-*

pity, and insane temper required by the character, both he and Kazan began looking for chinks in Griffith's psyche. Day after day, Griffith told Kazan the story of his life. Once, Kazan tried to goad him with "Remember all those people who said you'd never do anything about teach?"

"That doesn't bother me," Griffith told him desperately. "I'll tell you some things that do."

Andy told Kazan about being called "white trash" back in Mount Airy and that the phrase meant rejection to him. "Thereafter, Kazan would come up to Griffith on the set and whisper 'white trash' at him," Millstein wrote. Kazan realized that Andy had self-esteem problems, insecurity about his rural roots and worries, despite his college education, that his intellect was lacking. At one point, he had some of Andy's fellow cast members mock him for his alleged ignorance. "It's wrong, it's wrong," Andy told Millstein, "but thank goodness we found something I could use it in."

Millstein continued, revealing the mind games the character was playing with Andy at home:

> [In] *New York, in an ungovernable fury, he smashed three closet doors in his apartment. He did a great many other things, he said, but he would not specify what they were. "I did a lot of things to Barbara," he went on "mostly with silence. The thing was, I actually felt the power of Lonesome Rhodes. I'll tell you the truth: You play an egomaniac and paranoid all day and it's hard to turn it off by bedtime. We went through a nightmare—a real, genuine nightmare, both of us."*

In the last scene, Lonesome Rhodes is exposed as a fraud by his former girlfriend, played by Patricia Neal in a lead role. Lonesome thinks he's off the air, but she secretly flips a switch and puts him back on as he calls his fans "morons," saying, "Good night, you stupid idiots. Good night, you miserable slobs."

Kazan worried that Andy was too nice to pull off his character's response to being exposed and said he gave him "the Jack Daniels technique," getting him drunk for real. Rhodes drunkenly rages around his New York penthouse, at one point singing the gospel standard "Just a Closer Walk with Thee."

Millstein reported:

> *"When they shot that speech," [Andy] said, "I told 'em, 'Bring me some chairs, any old chairs around.' And I stomped 'em to pieces. It was pathetic.*

For a few minutes, I didn't even know it was me—trying to be this man."
The shot was silent except for the crack of wood breaking and splintering,
and Griffith's labored breathing. (Although he is big, Griffith is no athlete,
and he has not had a fistfight, he noted, since he was eight years old.)

"I had to grow up," Andy told Millstein. "I don't think I'll ever have that much trouble again. I'll be able to lead two lives."

Ron Howard said: "I don't think Andy liked facing that side of himself."

⸻

A Face in the Crowd came out in May 1957. Andy made a triumphant return to downtown Manteo for the local premiere, posing outside the venerable Pioneer Theater as his buddy Aycock Brown snapped photos of Andy "helping" the owners of the theater, the Creefs, put his name on their marquee. Andy, in an open-collared shirt, long pants and shoes, shoes rare for him on the island, smiles, posing beside posters of his raging character, seemingly leaving the darkness of the filming behind.

Over the next few years, Andy and Barbara would outfit Mountain Hill Farm as their own, the place, in the summers, they would start to raise their two adopted children, Sam and Dixie, and entertain their friends and their friends' children.

But Andy's work kept them in California for most of the year. Andy bought his parents, Carl and Geneva, known as "Nanny" to her grandchildren, a home near his in Los Angeles and would have them visit on the island. The islanders loved them all. "We were considered honorary locals," Dixie remembered.

A friend remembered the layout of the Griffith homestead:

It was a long and narrow house. To the west were three bedrooms and one bath. At the very end, off the master bedroom, was a glassed-in sunroom primarily used as the TV room and a place to send the children. To the east, the sound-side, and attached to the kitchen, was the secondary entrance, two maids' rooms and a laundry room.

A large dining room, furnished with Danish Modern pieces, open to the living room, was off to the side. The kitchen was mid-century modern, with wallpaper of bright blue and yellow, big enough for a table and chairs for the children.

47

Left: Andy at the Pioneer Theater in 1957 getting ready for the premiere of *A Face in the Crowd*. *Photo by Aycock Brown via Outer Banks History Center, State Archives of North Carolina.*

Below: Another shot of Andy at the *Face in the Crowd* premiere. *Photo by Aycock Brown via Outer Banks History Center, State Archives of North Carolina.*

Left: Andy's first wife, Barbara, with their son, Sam, in their Roanoke Island home in the late 1950s. *Photo by Aycock Brown via the Outer Banks History Center, State Archives of North Carolina.*

Right: Another shot of Sam. *Photo by Aycock Brown via the Outer Banks History Center, State Archives of North Carolina.*

Andy, a product of his times, would later hang a portrait of Civil War generals in the house, even as he became increasingly progressive in his politics. He and Barbara covered the walls of the phone room with photos of them, framed playbills of *No Time for Sergeants* and photos of Andy with various celebrities.

There was plenty of space for Andy's musical instruments, his guitars and his trombone, and his favorite rocking chair in the living room, with a big ashtray beside it for his Marlboros. Andy would relax there with friends, playing his favorite music on a turntable, his eclectic tastes ranging from jazz to country.

This was Andy's haven, proof that he had made it, and made it on his own. In a *Virginian-Pilot* newspaper photo taken soon after he and Barbara moved into the house, Andy is laid back in the rocking chair by the loaded ashtray, holding one of his dogs, his hair unruly, smiling wildly and proudly in an open-collared shirt and khakis and, of course, barefoot. He is in-your-face-cool, the Venetian blinds carefully set so the sun does not distract from the star.

In the years ahead, Andy would shop for antiques for the house. He had a good eye for them, as well as paintings and all kinds of clocks. An amateur woodworker, he fashioned lamps out of driftwood he and friends gathered. Following Skipper Bell's lead, Andy would closely supervise the planting of thousands of flowers in grass carefully planted and nurtured in the sand.

Through 1957 and most of 1958, Andy rode his growing fame. But *A Face in the Crowd*, while artistically brilliant, fizzled in box-office sales. Fans who'd loved Andy in the TV and Broadway versions of *No Time for Sergeants* and the 1958 film version couldn't get Lonesome Rhodes. Andy would later tell entertainment reporter Tim Clodfelter of the *Winston-Salem Journal* that an aunt of his, after watching a Piedmont, North Carolina premiere, came up to him and fussed, saying, "Andy, don't play mean!" Andy mimicked her sweet Southern voice as he laughed.

The criticism from near and far wasn't stopping Andy. He met former president Harry Truman and emceed the Azalea Festival in Wilmington, North Carolina, a big deal in the state.

Andy with North Carolina native David Brinkley, who was just starting *The Huntley-Brinkley Report* on NBC; former president Harry Truman; and Emma Neal Morrison, the chairwoman of the organization that puts on *The Lost Colony*, in the late 1950s. *Photo by Aycock Brown via Outer Banks History Center, State Archives of North Carolina.*

Above: In March
1958, Andy emceed
the Azalea Festival
in Wilmington,
North Carolina. This
photo foreshadows
Andy and Barbara's
growing discomfort
with being
beleaguered by fans.
*North Carolina Museum
of History.*

Right: Andy on the
set of *Onionhead. Outer
Banks History Center, State
Archives of North Carolina.*

All the while, Andy had been working on another film, *Onionhead*, a comedy-drama about characters on a U.S. Coast Guard ship during World War II. The decent cast included Ainslie Pryor, as well as Walter Matthau, who'd also been in *A Face in the Crowd*, and Joey Bishop.

Pryor had risen fast since leaving Raleigh in 1953, playing roles in eleven films. *Onionhead* was his last. On May 27, 1958, Pryor died in California of cancer. He was thirty-seven years old. Andy was crushed.

That October, *Onionhead* premiered. It got nowhere at the box office, a gut-punch to Andy following the poor reception of *A Face in the Crowd* and a punch to the memory of his friend Ainslie.

Andy's mercurial charge to the top that had begun just six years before with his comedic breakthrough at the Shrine Club in Nags Head was crashing. He was no longer making it in music, Broadway or movies. Andy was mourning Ainslie and anxious. "He was my best friend until he died," Andy would later say.

An island friend offered these thoughts on Andy's mindset at the time:

> *It seems to me his reaction to criticism was to rather quietly internalize it, convert it into determination, and prove it wrong by any means necessary. That is not to say he did not "get hot as hell"; he had quite a temper! But it was most always the result of not getting his way, someone not doing what he wanted them to do, when he wanted it done.*
>
> *I think both these behaviors were learned early in his life. As a child, he must have had an "I'll show you attitude," and, at home, his sweet mother always let him have his way. Whenever he did not get his way, he was finished with the person who got in his way.*

3

DRAWING ISLAND STRENGTH
FOR THE START OF THE AG SHOW

I think the year that really did it [1959] was the one year I had made, by now,
three motion pictures and my third one was a real turkey called Onionhead.
And I couldn't get a job for about a year. And so we stayed down here, Barbara
and I stayed here for about a year.
—Andy in the interview with David Stick,
describing how he came to be accepted by the islanders

*I*n 1959, Andy and Barbara retreated to the island. They would stay for a year, the longest span they were there in their marriage. From their island home, Andy would work the phone and fly out to Hollywood, trying to map his next move as sure as his fishing captain friends were mapping theirs.

Andy and Barbara renewed and enhanced ties with island friends. They joined Manteo's Mount Olivet United Methodist Church and its choir. "For one solid year I was the choir director in that church, and I had a church full of singers....We had a pretty good choir for a little town," Andy would tell David Stick.

Andy and Barbara had fun in church and outside it. Among some local men, there were regular card games, but Andy rarely took part. He couldn't be the center of attention in a card game, one local wryly explained.

The Griffiths partied with island friends, including the Harveys, the Wilsons and the Basnights. Another couple they were tight with was Wayland Fry and his wife, Dotty. Dotty, part of the Basnight family, was a long-legged, fun-loving beauty who had been a favorite model of Aycock Brown. Her husband was a World War II vet and popular teacher and coach at Manteo High School. The Frys had recently built a cottage at South Nags Head. Andy and Barbara would sometimes visit them there, playing the piano and drinking.

Other times, Andy and Barbara would join friends in riding up the beach to Nags Head, dining at the Arlington and dancing at the bar in the Carolinian Hotel, a majestic, flat-topped building of stone that shimmered out of the blond dunes like something out of old Cuba. The folks who ran the oceanfront hotel catered to their fellow aristocracy from northeastern North Carolina, as well as the folks from Manteo and tourists who came to the hotel bar to hear live music. In those days before liquor by the drink, brown-bagging ruled, with patrons bringing in their favorite booze and paying a setup fee, a couple of dollars for ice, mixer and glasses. Patrons would spill out of the bar and fall into rattan sofas in the hallways to snuggle. The knotty pine walls of the old hotel held their secrets.

Andy bought a fine sixteen-foot boat, clean-lined of wood with an Evinrude outboard engine, constructed by local boatbuilder John Allen and Andy's island friend Jack Wilson, for outings on the Sound. He named it *The Playboy*.

Then Andy discovered pontoon boats, which had been invented up in Minnesota in 1951. These boats rest on hollow metal cylinders that, appropriately, look like elongated beer kegs, for the boats are stable platforms in calm waters for partying, seating several passengers on soft cushions. They are ugly and slow but draw little water, sometimes less than a foot, which minimizes the chance of grounding and eases docking.

Andy's pontoon boat became his local trademark. "We laughed at the boat," said one of his closest friends. "But I will give him this: It was probably one of the first pontoon boats on the island, and many more followed."

For the lucky souls who go in boats, their preferred watercraft says volumes about them. Andy, who could have had any boat he wanted, chose a humble one built for fun, a homely but sturdy craft with plenty of room for his local friends, an escape from the hard false glitter of stardom.

In 1960, Andy began to push his way back to the top, starting with a lead-in as a small-town sheriff in an episode of the popular *Danny Thomas Show*. Andy's own namesake show premiered on CBS prime time on October 3,

1960, which just happened to be the birthday of novelist Thomas Wolfe, the most famous of the Carolina Playmakers, the group Andy had performed with back at Chapel Hill. In the runup to the premiere, entertainment writer Mal Vincent of the *Virginian-Pilot* newspaper in Norfolk, who'd graduated from Carolina a few years after Andy, wrote that Andy had sold out to TV. Andy called Vincent, who would write about their chat years later:

> *"Maaal," he grunted into the telephone. "It's Andy, Andy Griffith down Manteo way." This was the way he always greeted you, and it was always followed by a long pause. Eventually, he added, "Mal, I haven't sold out. You know, this is a job, and you take the jobs you get. This show won't last. I'll be back in movies."*

The pressure was on Andy. In his view, he'd fizzled on Broadway and in Hollywood, so TV was his last resort.

But there would be nothing like Andy's show, Ron Howard told the author in 2021. There was the classic humor, once Andy enlisted Don Knotts as his deputy during that first year. The humor blended with Sheriff Taylor's gentle lessons about loving and uplifting neighbors. Andy never took a writing credit on the show, but he and Don met weekly with the writers, giving much input. Andy told Howard he "never wanted to write" but he did "like to talk."

"Andy took a lot of pleasure in working with the writers and delivering ideas that way," Howard said. "He was a great natural leader on the show. He had a temper, but he didn't show it very much on the set."

Andy and Don, both from small-town, working-class backgrounds (Don from West Virginia), became fast friends. Andy called Don "Jess," his play on Don's first name, Jesse, and Don called Andy "Ange" the latter a habit that quickly carried over into the show. Andy Griffith soon became Sheriff Taylor. "You're supposed to believe in the character," Andy told the *New York Times*. "You're not supposed to think, 'Gee, Andy's acting up a storm.'"

By the time Andy signed this photo for his goddaughter Bea Bell, he was cutting back on autographs, so he wrote on it "'ppreciate it, Bea," as in she *better* appreciate it. *Courtesy Bea Bell.*

Andy sprinkled Roanoke Island names throughout the show. Sheriff Taylor referred to "Doc Harvey," a nod to his buddy W.W. Harvey, Manteo's only doctor, a beloved islander. A bank robbery conspirator posing as a photographer introduced himself as "Joe Layton," a shoutout to the great director of *The Lost Colony* during that time. A young girl with blond hair was referred to as "Claudia," which just happened to be the name of an island friend of Andy's daughter with blond hair. Otis the town drunk may have gotten his first name from the old name of a cove near Andy's island property.

Andy and Barbara, during their early years of going for broke across North Carolina with their singing/comedy act, had a pact: Whichever one made it big first, the other would step back and play a supporting role. It's questionable whether Andy would have taken the subordinate role. Andy had Barbara on his show once, in 1964. She made a cameo appearance as a member of the Mayberry choir. Barbara, without work to stabilize her, was drinking hard. That caused fights between the two of them. Andy was drinking hard, too, but he was the star, and males ruled in the 1960s.

4

DREAMS RISING AND FALLING

s the AG show took off, Andy's pressures mounted. He knew his talent was a gift but also believed acting was a trade and referred to it as such in interviews, a job he worked at just as hard as his father had labored in the factory, just as hard as his friends on the island labored aboard their boats and in their shops. His toil just came with a different price. Arriving before daybreak at the set, Andy would often first visit with his psychiatrist, forever trying to resolve the self-esteem problems from his hometown. Sometimes, he once said, he would get neck tension so bad he couldn't turn his head: "Then I knew I was in trouble."

There was another tension: Andy was naïve with women. In high school, girls had looked down on him. He wasn't an athlete, and he was blue-collar. With Barbara, he had found a good woman who loved him for who he was. But as Andy became a star, other women were coming at him. Andy didn't know how to handle it, one island friend said. He had affairs during the 1960s, some say, although others say he did not.

In a 1964 episode of the AG show, "Prisoner of Love," Sheriff Taylor is almost seduced by a beguiling blond jewel thief whom out-of-town lawmen have asked him to hold in the Mayberry jail. In uncharacteristic dramatic moments, Andy's facial gestures skillfully portray the struggle he faces.

Barbara and the children spent summers on the island. Andy, restricted by his show schedule, was there for most of August.

He and Barbara would load the pontoon boat with food, friends, booze and, for the children, sodas. "Dad would say, 'Get a crowd together for the boat,'" Dixie remembered. "It was a labor of love to create a day of waterskiing and volleyball and food for a large group. Dad loved to say how it took a whole lot of work for a little bit of fun. It was well worth the efforts involved by all. I loved it when Dad would allow me to helm the wheel of the boat. I felt so grown up!"

Dixie Griffith (*right*) and her friend Claudia Fry Sluder Harrington by the Sound near the Griffith house in 1968. *Courtesy Claudia Fry Sluder Harrington.*

In a home movie from the time, Andy is at the helm, wearing sunglasses and a nerdy button-up sweater. Barbara is near him in her own shades, beautifully cool. Andy smiles, turning on his Sheriff Taylor persona as he watches over the laughing children, all blond, his own and those of his island friends Jack Wilson and Doc Harvey.

"I remember most fondly the times I shared alone with my dad," Dixie said. "Running errands around town, be it Fearing's drug store or R.D. Sawyer's car dealership, perhaps the Ben Franklin Five & Dime, or Kellogg Supply Co.

"Life on the island, and Dad's vast property, offered numerous opportunities, unlike the more cloistered restrictions of our California home. Dad taught Sam and me how to drive manual transmission vehicles—boats, tractors minibikes—and how to shoot at targets with shotguns and pistols."

Sheriff Taylor referred to alcohol as "hooch," "booze," "redeye" and "happy water," and its effects as "getting gassed," "buzzed" and "loaded," but rarely drank. Many drank hard on the island. Andy and Barbara were no exception. The Griffith house was one of several party spots.

Some tourists on U.S. 64 would slow down in front of the wooded entrance to Andy's estate, wanting to catch a glimpse of him. Occasionally, if a tourist would drive up Andy's long driveway, one islander remembered,

Andy would lean out of his front door with one of his shotguns and let go a skyward blast, just to scare them away. One night as Andy hustled toward the door to frighten the intruders, he fumbled and the gun went off into the floorboards of the house. The islander, who was a young child at the time watching TV in the house with other children as the adults drank and smoked, said his mother hustled him home, telling his father, "Get the baby. We're leaving."

Andy could be mercurial in all sorts of ways.

In an Aycock Brown photo, one of the rare ones where he snapped Andy off guard, Andy, Barbara and Skipper Bell are at a social setting. It is night. Andy and Barbara have drinks in their hands; Barbara has a cigarette, and Skipper has a cigar clenched in his lips, as always, unlit. Andy, in profile with a suit coat and a loosened tie, is talking, head down and stormy-faced as Barbara watches him closely, alluring and tense. Skipper, wearing glasses and his straw fedora, stares past them, maybe hoping to ignore the drama. One of Andy's best friends said, judging from Barbara's expression, she is bracing for a temper tantrum from Andy as she brings him some sort of bad news.

Andy; his first wife, Barbara; and his Manteo "godfather," Skipper Bell, in the early 1960s. *Aycock Brown photo, courtesy Quentin Bell.*

Ron Howard writes in his 2021 memoir *The Boys* that Andy was blunt about the injury that caused him to wear a cast on his right hand in a few episodes of the show, saying, "I got drunk, I got mad, and I put my fist through a door."

Andy's tight circle of locals knew that the tantrums he occasionally threw were outweighed by his good works. In 1967, he began giving back to the island, restarting the long-dormant Manteo High School band with the donation of thirty-three new instruments. He remembered what it was like when a Moravian preacher back in his hometown, the Reverend Ed Mickey, taught him to play trombone, starting his lifelong love of music. "It's a kick, it's fun, it's a thrill, and you're doing something, you're creating something, and it makes you feel wonderful," Andy would say in the David Stick interview.

For more than a decade, Andy paid the salary of Manteo High's band director, Winfred Simpson Sr.

"This became, though I had to work in New York and some in California, this became my home," Andy told Stick. "I heard about this band, about this Black guy that taught who was trying to start a little band....I asked him what he needed, come tell me what you need, and he told me what he needed and I got 'em....I never wanted anybody especially to know it. I didn't want to have anything to do with the band. I felt that if I tried to tell them how to run it, that would hurt it....The more activities that they can have in these schools, the better chance for these young people to find themselves."

Just as Andy had found himself on the island.

Johnnie Robbins Jr., a former Manteo High School principal, remembered that Andy's help for the band was key.

Andy did that push quietly. But he was beginning to realize the power his presence could bring to an Outer Banks cause through just a photo. In the fall of 1968, Andy knew that media attention was needed on the dredging of Oregon Inlet, the key passage for commercial fishing boats to the ocean. Federal money for the project was crucial. That October, Andy posed for a photo, apparently shot by Aycock Brown, of him, "Doc" Harvey and their sons outside the Oregon Inlet Coast Guard Station. The photo caption noted that Andy, "an avid boater," was "vitally interested" in the progress of the dredging of the inlet and was told after a visit to the project that the work was going well. "Andy (the Sheriff of Mayberry) was an instant hit among the men in the crew, numbering about 45," the caption noted.

The dredging was completed, perhaps spurred on Andy's support.

Barbara supported Andy in his giving back to the island. She was sweet, gentle and frustrated that she had given up her own show business career.

Andy, "Doc" Harvey and their sons at the Oregon Inlet Coast Guard Station in October 1968. *Coastland Times photo courtesy Elizabeth Granitzki.*

In 1968, Andy hit his own shoals as he ended the AG show, with the last episode having aired that April. The show went out at No. 1 in the Nielsen ratings. Ira David Wood III, who was playing Sir Walter and would go on to direct the play in the years ahead, remembers visiting Andy in the living room of his island home after the AG show ended. Andy, Wood said, was "in his cups," going through a stack of AG scripts:

> *He looked so depressed. "I can put my hands on $16 million today and I'm so unhappy," he said. I told him, "Andy, give me $1 million and I'll show you how to be ecstatic." I think he was worried that that when he went* [on TV talk shows], *people were laughing at him, not with him. I told him, "Andy, you're a legend, everybody loves you." Barbara walked me out, saying, "That's what he needed to hear. He loves you so much, and I do, too."*

It was vintage Barbara, lovingly supportive of Andy and his friends.

Dixie remembers a summer afternoon in 1970. "Dad was itching to get out of the house and take a motorcycle ride. I happened to be nearby. He told me, 'Grab a helmet and hop on! He revved up the bike, I got on the back, and off we went. We went so fast across the Manns Harbor bridge. It was pouring rain, windy and exhilarating. Later, I remember thinking how my mom would've had a fit had she known. This was close to the end of their marriage."

Andy and Barbara separated in 1971. One of Andy's close local friends blamed the split on Andy's manager Dick Linke, saying he had divorced his wife and encouraged Andy to do the same. Other islanders said Andy left Barbara over her drinking, even though he was drinking heavily as well. She would later quit.

Barbara was universally adored by islanders. They were sympathetic to her troubles with the bottle, one many of them knew well. One local fondly remembers Barbara patiently teaching him how to draw when he was a child. At one point, when Andy talked trash about Barbara, a local friend, Della Basnight, rebuked him and told him to stop doing that. Andy got mad but then complied. Andy loved Della because she could make him laugh.

5

NEW BEGINNINGS
IN THE SUMMER OF '72

For a long time, I was in comedy. Then around 1970 or 1971,
the kind of comedy I did fell out of fashion.
—Andy talking to a reporter in 1984

The image is one thing and the human being is another.
It's very hard to live up to an image, put it that way.
—Elvis Presley, 1972

They rolled north through southern Nags Head one evening in
June 1972 in Andy's red Ford Bronco, the windows down, the
ocean peeking through sea oats on low dunes on their right, the
sun setting on the Sound on their left. They sipped from their vodka tonics,
"travelers," the damp, salt-splashed wind blowing through their hair, hers
brunette, his gray-streaked brown, sneaking peeks at each other. Sue Guthrie
was twenty-five. Andy was forty-six.

Andy had recently separated from Barbara. Andy and Sue had met the
summer before when he and Barbara had dined with one of their fellow *Lost
Colony* vets, Floyd "Chunk" Simmons, and Sue, then a dancer in *The Lost
Colony*, at Spencer's, a restaurant on the Nags Head Causeway.

In the summer of '72, Andy and Sue renewed their acquaintance. Sue was
back at *The Lost Colony* as a dancer and working part-time for Edward Greene,
a fellow *Lost Colony* alum of Andy's, at the Christmas Shop in Manteo. Andy

Left: Andy clowning with Susan Guthrie "Sue" Lowrance in a montage of photos from the 1970s, including the summer of 1972. *Courtesy Susan Guthrie Lowrance.*

Below: Andy poses for a photo backstage at *The Lost Colony* in the late 1950s. *Aycock Brown photo, Outer Banks History Center, State Archives of North Carolina.*

Above, left: Andy and fellow actor Floyd "Chunk" Simmons during a day off from *The Lost Colony* in the early 1950s. *Photo by Aycock Brown via Outer Banks History Center, State Archives of North Carolina.*

Above, right: Andy speaking backstage at *The Lost Colony* in the 1970s. *Roanoke Island Historical Association archives.*

Right: Andy backstage at *The Lost Colony. Aycock Brown photo, Outer Banks History Center, State Archives of North Carolina.*

would visit back backstage at the pageant before the show began, pulling up in a small motorboat behind the waterfront set, talking to Sue and the rest of the cast before the show started. "He was very open, quick-witted and lots of fun," Sue, now Susan Guthrie Lowrance, remembered.

Andy invited Sue and other *Lost Colony* friends out on his pontoon boat on Sundays, the daylight hours leading up to the one night of the week the show took a break. The friends waterskied in the Sound, then anchored at sand spits and played volleyball and picnicked, the sandwiches, chips and ice-cold beer especially tasty in the salt air. They laughed and played until they ran out of provisions or until a summer rain cloud became too threatening.

Sue, in graduate school at the University of North Carolina–Greensboro, was a shapely former beauty queen and physical education teacher from New Jersey with big brown eyes and thick dark brown hair, warm and welcoming.

As they cruised the two-lane Beach Road, Andy wore an open-collared shirt and khakis, characteristically rolled up to his calves above his bare feet to feel the breeze and be ready to wade in the Sound or sea. He was belting out "I'll Fly Away" and other gospel songs. In between verses, he and Sue laughed. She was infatuated with Andy. "I couldn't believe it," she remembers. "It was like being in a movie.'"

Sue had never met anybody like Andy. "He was constantly studying people, finding humor in everyday stuff," she said. "Sometimes he would see silly behavior that would make him laugh so hard he would almost cry."

A decade earlier, when Sue was a young teenager, Andy had drawn from Roanoke Island characters, as well as ones he'd known growing up in Mount Airy, to turn his namesake show into a prime-time hit. In Manteo, he'd absorbed the give-and-take chats of islanders and their subtle changes in tone, from serious to wisecracking. He had taken in their body language, sometimes slouching, sometimes shoulders-thrown-back proud, and their eyes, sometimes rolling, sometimes pop-eyed, and the way they walked with their friends and children, sometimes lightly touching arms, other times drawing away.

He poured it all into the characters on his show, most notably by working with Don Knotts as the goofy Deputy Barney Fife. Andy played the straight man to Don, realizing that made the show work and brought in the money, subordinating the lead comedic role that would have been the most artistically challenging and fun to him. The show, while escapist, had touched a deep chord, that of Americans wanting to forget the Vietnam War and race riots and embrace supposedly simpler times, when a savvy sheriff who rarely packed a gun solved his small town's problems and played a compassionate straight man to Barney and the rest of the townsfolk. "The show reflected the North Carolina of Andy's childhood, even though things looked fairly contemporary," Ron Howard told the author. "In his mind, it really reflected an earlier time." The cars were of the 1960s and a few years before, but the phones were old-timey and so was much of the show's feel, idealized small-town sensibilities.

In 1965, Don left for a lucrative Hollywood film contract, and the fun of the show left for Andy. He loved Don, but his competitive side was uncomfortable with his friend's success. As the series went from black and white to color that year, Andy deflated. He seemed restrained, subdued and bored. In the black-and-white shows, Andy had occasionally segued into the soliloquy style that had made him famous, riffing off *Romeo and Juliet* and spinning "The Shot Heard 'Round the World" tale as he explained things to Opie. He often played his guitar. Most of that was gone with the color shows in the late 1960s.

A random glimpse of those shows might evoke a comforting Norman Rockwell painting, and ratings were still good, but the star had faded. Andy, who told a reporter in the late 1950s that there was no point in trying to dispense with his Southern drawl, had been toning it down throughout the series. In the last episodes, he really left it behind, his accent going from one of "worryin', tryin'" and "ain'ts" to one of "worrying and trying" and "are nots," the foothills boy awkwardly trying on a city slicker style. "He felt stymied, handcuffed, stereotyped," Della Basnight, an actress herself, remembered. "That is why he was messing around with his voice on the show. He was looking for something, anything, to break through to something else."

Ron Howard said the color shows "became a little less aggressively funny. They didn't have Don's genius in the center of it. Without a doubt, the show was never as much fun for Andy after Don left."

Regarding Andy's accent, he said, "I think Andy was looking to the future and really wanting Mayberry and the South to be viewed in a slightly more contemporary way, more relatable. He didn't want to go to 'No Time for Sergeants.' He was looking ahead to his acting career."

Some viewers of the black-and-white shows might have found it easy to accept that the show was not taking on contemporary issues. But when the show went color, that absence was glaring.

It was amazing that a show about a North Carolina sheriff had been a prime-time hit. Andy knew that. To Ron Howard's point, Andy was conscious of how his state was being presented to the nation, especially as other sitcoms about rural characters came out. Andy expressed disapproval about one script for his show, saying, "We're not *The Beverly Hillbillies.*"

In some dining scenes in the last years of his show, Andy, the gap in his front teeth professionally closed, primly keeps his left hand in his lap. His handlers had long since tamed his rowdy pompadour. Andy's longtime manager, Dick Linke, who had once encouraged Andy to embrace his rural image, reversed, telling one associate in 1970: "Don't use those old pictures of Andy for publicity, they make him look like the goofball he used to be; now he's a very modern guy, mature and articulate."

It was as if Andy was trying to emulate Ainslie Pryor, chasing his ghost. Andy had written in liner notes for a 1959 album, *Andy Griffith Shouts the Blues and Old Timey Songs*, that Ainslie was brilliant and "helped me in the beginning in whatever career I've got more than anybody else." Andy's other alter ego from the Colony days, Bob Armstrong, was soaring in Hollywood, a go-to character actor, having worked his way up from spots on Andy's show and TV westerns such as *Gunsmoke* and *The Big Valley* to become a favorite of the avant-garde Western director Sam Peckinpah. Andy would call Bob and Don and talk about the good times, but it was cold comfort. They were rising, and he was falling. Don had yet to visit the island, and Bob had never returned. Jack Dodson, a good friend and partier, in sharp contrast to his straight-laced Howard Sprague role on Andy's show, did visit Andy on the island, but it was not the same.

By the summer of '72, Andy's namesake show was four years in the rear-view mirror and he was in the process of divorcing Barbara. He'd brought his friend Aneta Corsaut to the island once, but she left early. Andy's teenage son, Sam, told a friend that she didn't like sand or water, so his father sent her packing. Corsaut was not a beach person, but it's questionable whether Andy gave her a rude sendoff.

He wanted to rekindle the dramatic artistry he'd had in *A Face in the Crowd*. Andy had gone for the bucks with his show, shucking off the dramatic side he was now trying to revive. But he was stereotyped as Sheriff Taylor, not making it in films or TV, even as actors who'd had some of their first roles in his show, including Jack Nicholson, were ascending. Andy didn't want to end up like Orson Welles, an early legend washing up like a bloated flounder on TV talk shows.

"When you make your primary mark in situation comedy, it's a double-edged sword in terms of people's expectations of you as an artist and a persona for years to come," Ron Howard said.

Andy loved his work. He hated not working. He worried about money. Andy and Dick Linke had owned half of the AG show but sold the rerun rights, an eventual cash cow. As Andy's divorce from Barbara became final in 1972, the court reportedly determined that Andy was worth about $7 million, about $47 million in 2022 dollars, and gave Barbara half. Andy was not happy to surrender that amount. But he was more worried about his acting.

His triumphs in drama *and* comedy were rare in the 1960s, with only Jackie Gleason coming close, setting the stage for Whoopi Goldberg and Tom Hanks in the 1980s. Andy's fellow Southern artist Harper Lee published one great novel, *To Kill a Mockingbird*, in 1960 (the same year Andy debuted Sheriff Taylor) and would not publish another book in her lifetime. Andy had, in the Hemingway parlance, knocked out his competitors and done it by the time he was only forty.

But it was not enough. Craig Fincannon, who had gotten to know Andy while working in *The Lost Colony* in college in the 1970s and was later the location casting director for *Matlock*, said that Andy "wanted more. He wanted to be tested."

In the summer of 1972, Andy was back on his island, taking a break. This was home. On the rare occasions when he had to go back to his native town, Mount Airy, he got a tight spot in his chest, he told a friend, remembering being called "white trash" there.

The island was where he belonged. He loved walking around Manteo barefoot, relishing the busyness of town and the windswept beauty of the surrounding marshes and shimmering waters. Islanders protected his privacy, not telling the tourists where he lived. The locals didn't judge him, and he didn't judge them. "Everybody on this island wants to know everything about their neighbors, but nobody cares," one of Andy's close friends said. "Nobody's passing judgment. All we want to know is what you want to drink,"

The friend said Andy was "a hard-partying workaholic and extremely insecure. He was definitely damaged by being called 'white trash' growing up, especially by the girl in his class when was twelve or thirteen. He really internalized that, it hurt him deeply. He spent his life trying to overcome it."

In an Aycock Brown photo of the opening of a local bank branch in downtown Manteo in the summer of 1969, Andy is shielded by shades, signing an autograph for a local woman and her two boys in tank tops. She, too, wears shades, arms folded, unsmiling, watching Andy for more. Andy just scribbles intently, looking down at the page, not making eye contact with the woman or her boys as a bank official by his side smiles at them.

Andy signing autographs at the opening of an East Carolina Bank branch in Manteo in the summer of 1969. *Aycock Brown photo, Outer Banks History Center, State Archives of North Carolina.*

On the island, Andy didn't have to worry about getting in trouble or bad press. It was his place for "cuttin' loose." Dare County sheriff Frank Cahoon was a friend, one who drove a Ford patrol car, like the one Sheriff Taylor had driven. Cahoon, like Sheriff Taylor but older, rarely wore a gun.

Another friend was Francis Meekins, the publisher of the local newspaper, the *Coastland Times.* Andy often stopped by Meekins's downtown office to swap gossip. One of the paper's most controversial and popular features, usually written by reporter Gaylord Godwin but unsigned, was a court report that detailed, with names of locals and tourists, travails ranging from drunken driving cases to fistfights. Andy was never in it.

His local friends knew that he valued loyalty, liked to be the center of attention and was competitive as all get out. His temper occasionally ran hot. But friends knew none of that was surprising for someone in his line of work.

His friends knew about taking chances, rising and falling. They knew about early promise unfulfilled. They knew about going through rough patches. He loved going back to his island core, the youngest and best of him, where all

Andy with Dare County sheriff Frank Cahoon, on his right, and Julian Oneto of the Carolinian Hotel in Nags Head. *Victor Meekins Papers, Outer Banks History Center, State Archives of North Carolina.*

was tied to *The Lost Colony*. When Andy went to the Manteo liquor store, he could chat with Robert Midgett, the store supervisor, who had been in the pageant in Andy's first years when they both played soldier roles, as Midgett carefully placed Andy's choice in a brown paper bag. Midgett, a barrel-chested man who loved belting out opera songs, was nicknamed "Singin' Bob," to distinguish him from other Robert Midgetts on the island, where many shared the same names.

Andy hung out with *Lost Colony* crew members, inviting them on his pontoon boat. He was trying to be hip, with his skinny legs and his worn Jantzen swimming trunks pulled up over his slight beer gut.

"Andy was extremely competitive at volleyball," Della Basnight remembered. "He would cuss us out, calling us 'Lost Colony idiots.' He was just competitive in general. You cannot be a passive person in his line of work."

Andy was no athlete, sometimes tripping over his size 12 feet, but that didn't stop his drive. Ira David Wood figured out a way to beat Andy during one epic game: Wood and his team cut back on the Bloody Marys that Andy freely served from pitchers before the game and during it.

———— ∞ ————

Andy missed the old days, when he could roam the island and beach free of autograph seekers. Sometimes, he would, perhaps inadvertently, signal his star status, like the first time he met Gary Oliver of the old Island Marina on the Causeway. Oliver heard someone whistling the theme from the AG show, looked outside, saw a man docking his pontoon boat, and asked him if he was Andy Griffith. "Yeah," Andy replied. Oliver let it go at that, and Andy became a regular customer, gassing up at the marina, buying outboard motors from him and shooting the breeze about the weather and local folks. Andy often had beauties on his boat, Oliver remembered.

At times, Andy would get mad if he wasn't recognized. But, for the most part, he was becoming increasingly guarded. Visiting his friends John and Elsie May Bell's supermarket in Nags Head, Andy would sometimes pull the hood of a green raincoat over his face so he wouldn't be recognized, Eddie Miller, then a teenager working at the store and now the owner of the hotel the Bells started, the Outer Banks Motor Lodge, remembers. Andy couldn't even go to a cocktail party without attracting attention, although he was still sometimes good-natured about it. At a party in Kill Devil Hills in the 1970s, Andy was drinking with friends on a sun deck as some of their children bounced up and down on a nearby trampoline, making a game of it, shouting "Andy, Andy!" He smiled and waved at them, one of the children, Bennett Rose Payne, remembered.

Andy, with a good eye for art, loved paintings, and often stopped by Ann and Jack Sandbergs' gallery in a former boathouse at the First Colony Inn in Nags Head. Jack's son, Eric, remembered the first time Andy came in: "I was probably twelve and had seen every episode of his show twice already. Being a dumb, overly excited kid, I ran up to the hotel and told everyone I saw that Andy was in the gallery. I remember seeing him walk back to his car, holding a bag, keys in hand, suddenly accosted by a gaggle of girls shoving pens and paper at him."

Later, when the Sandbergs moved the business farther north in Nags Head and opened the Yellowhouse Galleries on the Beach Road, Andy would often stop in, buying Ann's paintings of cottage rows and beachscapes. But Andy, Eric Sandberg said, spent most of his time in their antique print section, buying a lot of old maps and prints, with a particular interest in old prints related to slavery.

Ann Sandberg, now Ann Holland, remembered a day when Andy was browsing in the gallery and tourists kept stealing glances and whispering to each other, knowing he was "somebody" but not exactly sure who. Finally, Andy humbly told them, "I used to be on *The Andy Griffith Show*."

Sometimes, Andy would hop on one of his motorbikes and roar around the wooded trails on his property, just another islander trying out his wheels and guts. It might have been hard for him to know who he really was anymore, weighing the line between the foothills boy he'd been against the star he'd become, maybe missing the time when he was just another face on the island. In several episodes of the AG show, Andy flipped the mirror as the show tackled the ill effects of would-be stardom on Mayberry and its residents, most notably in "The Taylors in Hollywood" episodes of 1965, in which the sheriff, Aunt Bee and Opie visit Hollywood as a movie is being made about "the sheriff without a gun."

In real island time, locals tried to keep Andy in line. Once, he stopped by the oceanfront Sea Ranch hotel in Kill Devil Hills to pick up one of their chocolate chess pies and came in barefoot, Margo Blakely remembered. Alice Sykes, the legendary owner/operator of the hotel, told Andy, who was heavily intoxicated, to put some shoes on. Andy said he didn't have any. Miss Alice told him to "get the hell out." Andy left.

One night at Spencer's Restaurant on the Causeway, Andy and several other boozed-up buds were eating dinner. Andy, always a loud and aminated talker, was telling stories, waving his long arms around, nearly crashing his wingspan into waiters hustling by, balancing loaded food trays. The waiter for his table had introduced himself several times by name, but Andy kept calling him "boy." The waiter had shoulder-length hair, and one of Andy's friends asked loudly if the waiter was a boy or a girl, a common insult of those times.

Other waiters, including one at the Seafare in Nags Head, encountered a charming Andy. "Whenever he came in, he picked his own table, and all the waiters with tables available waited with great excitement to see if he would pick one of ours," Joseph Blount "Joe" Cheshire V remembered. "He was always nice and engaging and usually left a $100 tip, which in those days was real money," said Cheshire, who went on to become a noted criminal defense attorney in North Carolina.

On his best days, Andy would take his boat out to dream and think. The Sound offered freedom and beauty, far freer than Myers Lake of the AG show. He learned how to read the water, to follow the colors that marked its shallows and depths and to follow the seagulls and pelicans to where the fish were.

———— ∞∞∞ ————

To Sue Guthrie, Andy was downright romantic with his warm Southern charm.

"When he smiled at me and held me in his arms, I melted," she said. "I knew that we shared something special."

They rode up the Beach Road that evening, through the desolate Epstein tract, undeveloped sand owned by out-of-towners. They arrived at the restaurant in the Hayman family's Arlington in Nags Head. The hotel was near the start of "The Unpainted Aristocracy," a necklace of oceanfront cottages named for their unpainted cedar-shake siding, the second homes of the planter class from northeastern North Carolina, many of whom sent their boys to Andy's alma mater, the University of North Carolina. They had pledged fraternities and lived a privileged campus life as Andy had struggled just to pay his tuition. Now he had more money than many of them.

Phoebe Hayman greeted Andy and Sue at the door. She was short and graceful, her brown hair swept up in a tight bun over her fine facial bones. She escorted the couple in, past diners who stared wide-eyed at Andy. They knew better than to rise and try to greet him. They knew Phoebe was quick to give a warning stare to keep them at bay. Andy had learned how to turn on his own icy stare.

Phoebe seated the couple at a table for two with an ocean view of children playing in the sand and seagulls soaring in the twilight. A waiter quickly came to their table. The Arlington's Black waiters, dressed in short white tuxedo coats and black pants, were the best in the business, tired of the segregated South but knowing just when to talk to their white patrons and just when to back off, charming the tips that would send many of their children to college.

Andy and Sue talked, sharing the stories of their lives as they nibbled at fresh seafood. The flame in an oil lamp flickered between them.

Sue had grown up in New Jersey but had deep family roots on Roanoke Island. Her paternal grandparents were Elizabeth "Bettie" Midyette Guthrie and Captain Cecil Samuel Guthrie, who ran the mailboat from Manteo to Elizabeth City in the days before bridges connected the Outer Banks to the mainland. Sue often stayed in Manteo with her cousin Olga Creef, whose husband, George, ran the Pioneer Theater in Manteo, where Andy had gloried in the local premiere of *A Face in the Crowd* fifteen years ago.

In graduate school back in Greensboro, Sue was pursuing her Master of Fine Arts degree in dance. She was Andy's equal: bright, charming, smart and confident, striving to hone her artistic talent through *The Lost Colony*, just as Andy had done. In the summer of 1969, Sue toured Europe by herself for nine weeks, enriching her cultural quest for art, music and dance history. She loved artists who had achieved their dreams. Like Andy. She was the lift he needed. He listened intently, telling her he had never been to Europe, joking that she was "too worldly" for him.

Andy at the *Face in the Crowd* premiere at the Pioneer Theater in Manteo in 1957. *Photo by Aycock Brown via Outer Banks History Center, State Archives of North Carolina.*

Their meal over, they left the restaurant, Andy driving them back to Manteo and more romance. A couple of weeks later, as Barbara came to the island to stay at the Griffith homeplace on Roanoke Island for the rest of the summer, Andy rented a cottage in South Nags Head and invited Sue to join him. When she arrived, Andy had papers spread over the coffee table in the living room. He told her they were financial documents he was reviewing in advance of his divorce. "He was dealing with his L.A. attorney and many decisions," Sue said. "I respected his privacy."

As always, Andy made time for his children that summer. Dixie and Sam, carrying on their parents' tradition, took small parts in *The Lost Colony*, making their father proud. He knew they were safe under the watchful eyes of his old friends, costumer Renie Rains and actress Cora Mae Basnight (Della Basnight's mother) who had an iconic, humorous role as the Indian maiden Agona. Dixie, like her father, grew to love the creosote smell of the theater's old wood.

Andy also ran with his buddies. One of his best friends, Quentin Bell, was a son of Skipper Bell, Andy's "godfather" on the island.

Skipper had died several years before, and Andy "inherited" Quentin as one of his key confidants. Quentin was the manager of a paper company's vast holdings of pines and hardwood on mainland Dare County. He was tall and slim, soft-spoken, gentle and fun-loving. He had soundside land near Andy's. "Andy was a workaholic, and whenever he wasn't working, he would come here to the island," Quentin remembered. "He was friendly and affable, with his great sense of humor. He could describe some little situation, and there was a punchline. After Dad passed away, we would invite Andy to go on hunts. We became friends that way."

When he could get away from California in the fall, Andy began hunting with Quentin and other island friends. Once, Andy got the end of his shotgun barrel plugged with mud, causing the barrel to explode when he shot. But otherwise, Andy, whose sheriff character had occasionally shot

Andy with his old friend, *Lost Colony* costumer Renie Rains, holding the sword he used while playing Sir Walter. *Roanoke Island Historical Association archives.*

skeet and crows, knew his way around guns, preferring 12-gauge over/under shotguns on the show and in person. Over/unders were a variation on the old side-by-side style. They still had just two shots, a sporting option, but offered a single-barrel sighting plane, a favorite of skeet shooters and one just catching on among North Carolina hunters in the 1970s. Andy had won an over/under in a skeet-shooting competition in Mexico in 1966 and prized the shotgun with words about the win engraved on the receiver. But hunting with his island friends, Andy sometimes used a Remington 1100 semiautomatic shotgun.

"He was good with a shotgun, a wing shooter," Quentin said. "All of us locals had hunted since we were twelve or thirteen. We considered ourselves fairly good wing-shots, but Andy could hold his own. On duck hunts, we'd say 'There's a single coming in, take him Andy,' and he would usually get him on the first shot. There was nothing wrong with his marksmanship."

Andy, in a worn tan hunting coat and pants tucked into leather engineer boots, loved the boom of the shotguns, the sulphury smell of gun smoke and the camaraderie, trading stories with his buddies.

Andy, Quentin and their friends went on bird shoots in mainland Hyde County with a rich northerner who had bought up a large tract of land. Ken Mann, an island radio broadcaster, went along on one of the hunts. Unfortunately, he said, locals got wind that Andy was there. When they tried to have a quiet lunch in a remote barn, fans came in. Andy was not pleased.

Andy and Quentin Bell would charter boats for fishing in the Gulf Stream, a cool thirty-five-mile ride of two hours from the Outer Banks, into the pretty water where dolphins played and sharks sometimes cascaded against the catches, furies of water and blood. The captains of the charter boats, the "cappies," told wondrous stories that Andy filed away in his brain to use in his work.

Other days, Andy, Quentin and Doc Harvey would hop in Andy's Ford Bronco and ride across the bridge to the Dare County mainland, once taking along Aycock Brown and reveling in roadside wildflowers, at play in their fields.

Andy's other buddies around that time included John Bell (no relation to Quentin, but friends), who ran a supermarket in Nags Head and the Outer Banks Motor Lodge. John and his wife, Elsie May, a pianist and Juilliard grad, had been tight with Andy and Barbara, who were the godparents of their daughter, Bea. When the Bells were building their house in Nags Head in the late 1950s—when Bea was a baby—they lived in the Griffith house for six months, while Andy and Barbara were in California for much of that time.

On a northeastern North Carolina hunt, Andy played for the camera with a clutch of downed pigeons. *Courtesy Quentin Bell.*

Andy fixed a drink after the hunt was done. *Courtesy Quentin Bell.*

Andy fishing with one of his best island buddies, Quentin Bell, in the 1970s. *Courtesy Quentin Bell.*

The families had remained close, the Bells often visiting the Griffiths in their island home. Andy sometimes told ghost stories to Bea, Betsy Harvey and their friends when they were little, one story about a peg-legged man who supposedly lived nearby, just like Sheriff Taylor had done with Opie and his friends around a campfire in a 1964 episode of his show titled "Back to Nature"—scaring them, as well as Barney and Gomer, as he weaves a tale about a hermit with a golden arm. Bea and Betsy, now Elizabeth "Liz" Granitzki, remember the spellbinding modulation in Andy's voice as he told them stories, speaking softly, then building to a loud ending that had them shivering and shaking. "He'd get us scared, and then someone would turn the lights out," Bea said. "He had the gift of telling stories."

Elsie May Bell remained close with Barbara.

Andy's other partying friends were Tommy Daniels, who owned a popular department store in Manteo; Jimmy Austin, a commercial fisherman who ran a seafood store in Nags Head; and Fred Murray, who operated an auto supply store in Nags Head. One of Andy's best friends was Ray White. He shared with Andy and Quentin a love of good times and joking around. Ray was rising in the local banking business.

Above: Andy fishing off his island in the 1970s. *Courtesy Quentin Bell.*

Right: Andy tinkers with a camera on a boat outing in the 1970s. *Courtesy Quentin Bell.*

Quentin Bell, Andy and "Doc" Harvey at play in Dare County wildflowers in the 1970s.
Aycock Brown photo, courtesy of Elizabeth Granitzki.

Andy's goddaughter Bea
Bell, at play in his island
home in the late 1950s.
Courtesy Bea Bell.

Andy often stopped by the Manteo bank where Ray worked, leaving him a hamburger or hotdog for lunch. One Saturday, Andy and Ray drove up to Corolla, on the northern Outer Banks, in Andy's Bronco, drinking beer and watching wild horses descended from shipwreck survivors.

The week after the Corolla trip, Ray noticed he hadn't heard from Andy and asked his secretary about that. She said Andy had left him a sandwich in the breakroom. Ray eagerly opened the brown paper bag and unwrapped its contents, finding a nice sesame-seed bun with lettuce and tomato over a burger. Just as he was getting ready to bite, he took a closer look and realized the "burger" was horse manure that Andy had carefully saved from the previous weekend. Ray called Andy to let him know he'd met his joke. Andy laughed his ass off.

Andy loved to joke with, and sometimes play jokes on, his island friends. *Aycock Brown photo, Outer Banks History Center, State Archives of North Carolina.*

But Ray couldn't stop thinking: He would have eaten that turd if he hadn't realized what it was. Andy would have laughed even harder. On the set of his show, Andy had loved to play practical jokes on Don Knotts. Ray was his new foil.

Andy was one unequivocal soul. There was no gray among his likes and dislikes. If he liked someone, he said it loud, and vice versa, like when friends suggested people to join his party pontoon boat ventures. Of some candidates, he would say, "Oh hell yeah, I love him." Of others, he would say, "Hell no! That guy is never setting foot on my boat."

He could also be contradictory. He would spend time drinking with Jack Wilson and other friends at Jack's "hunting camp" on the Sound near Manteo. It was actually a house with three slot machines from Las Vegas, a big oak poker table and a fully stocked bar hidden behind a bookcase, a gun cabinet hidden behind another bookcase, and a bath with a saltwater shower. Jack would often say, "It sleeps six sober, but twenty-four drunk, so come on, we'll have fun."

Sometimes when Andy would return, he would rave about good times there. Other times, he would rage about the camp, saying he never wanted to go there again. On one outing there, Andy may have turned against it because he fell and cut his head open on a boat.

Sue, warm and friendly, balanced out Andy's occasional brooding side. He always made her feel extra special, she said.

Once, Andy took her to Raleigh as he filmed a commercial in the area for one of his business ventures, canned baked beans. They dined at the venerable Angus Barn steakhouse and lodged at the Velvet Cloak, a lazy lady of a hotel in the state capital, the name a nod to the legend of Sir Walter Raleigh throwing down his cloak over a street mud puddle to ease a lady's path. Andy, *The Lost Colony*'s most famous Sir Walter, would have winked at the history. Sue was totally smitten.

As *The Lost Colony* season ended, Andy headed back to California. As much as he loved the island, California was where he plied his trade. His creative drive would get "real hungry," he would say, and he had to return.

Sue returned to UNC Greensboro. In October, Andy flew her to Nashville to attend the Columbia Records Awards show. He was the master of ceremonies. Sue remembered Andy pacing back and forth in their hotel room before the country music event as he went over his lines, wanting, as always, to get his performance just right. He did fine, responding to applause with his trademark "'ppreciate it," adding, "Where I come from, if a fellow didn't like country music, they would think you were funny [strange]. But I'm alright because I like it."

Among the many stars in Nashville that weekend was pop crooner Andy Williams, a friend of Andy Griffith's, and Merle Haggard, whom Andy would later work with in a TV mini-series. In one photo, Andy, in a coat and tie, grins by a much shorter Johnny Paycheck, an original country outlaw known for his drunken antics offstage who would become famous in five years for his cover of "Take This Job and Shove It." Paycheck, in an uncharacteristic tux and looking surprisingly sober, smiles up admiringly at Andy.

Andy on a Gulf Stream fishing trip out of Oregon Inlet in the summer of 1972 with Susan Guthrie "Sue" Lowrance. *Courtesy Susan Guthrie Lowrance.*

Sue was hoping Andy would continue their relationship. But that was not part of his plan, as he had already met an alluring Greek actress in Los Angeles, Solica Cassuto. That summer, Andy's British housekeeper, Lillian "Lady" Hawkins, had befriended Sue and shared with her that Andy was dating someone in Los Angeles. "I think Lilian knew that I was falling in love with him, and she was trying to protect me from getting hurt," Sue said.

A few weeks after the Nashville trip, Sue received a handwritten letter from Andy. He wrote that he enjoyed the summer and the fun they had, but he was moving on with the woman he had met in California. Sue appreciated his honesty but was disappointed because she loved Andy.

In January 1973, Sue moved to Los Angeles to hone her skills in dance and theater. In February, the Arlington, where Sue and Andy had dined, surrendered to the sea, the victim of a mean nor'easter. "I remember hearing about it and thinking 'There go all those memories, out to sea,'" Sue said.

A beach friend had told her to look up Bob Armstrong, Andy's old friend from *The Lost Colony*, and gave her Armstrong's Los Angeles phone number. Sue called him. They began a wonderful friendship, and soon they were dating. "He was six-four and had this deep, mesmerizing voice like a Southern preacher," she said. "When he walked in a room, everything stopped."

At first, she and Armstrong spent a lot of time talking about Andy. Once, she said, Armstrong called Andy, telling him, "You really broke this girl's heart."

She ended up falling in love with Armstrong. "I could talk to him," Sue said. "It just gave me a comfort level, and a meaningful relationship evolved."

Armstrong studied the spiritual and esoteric writings of the philosophers Gurdjieff, Ouspenskii and Krishnamurti. He freely shared his knowledge with his family and friends. He also studied creative healing with Mabel Young and helped heal many friends, dancers and movie-set grips with his massage techniques. Ahead of his time, Armstrong had a reputation among his inner circle of friends for growing and curating his own marijuana garden

Andy with his second wife, Solica, on his right, and his island friend Lee Bell on his left.
Courtesy Quentin Bell.

for which he was proud, but private about sharing. It was not a business for Armstrong but part of his holistic healing process.

Andy was amazed by Bob's spiritual "book" knowledge. Bob's widespread friends in Hollywood included actors Bo Hopkins, Lony Chapman and Pat Hingle. Hingle had been on Andy's show and would become a favorite of Clint Eastwood in his films.

Sue and Armstrong married in 1973. Andy and Solica Cassuto married the same year.

Once, Sue and Bob went to a party at Andy's house in the Toluca Lake neighborhood of Los Angeles, a house that once belonged to Bing Crosby. "Don Knotts was there, and a Dixieland jazz band was playing in the living room," she said. "Don and I rolled up the carpet and we danced. He was a great dancer and fun. Another time, Bob and I were at Andy's and Andy told us all to grab an old hat off the hat rack. We put them on. Then Andy, leading us in gospel songs, drove us through Forest Lawn cemetery in his Model-A Ford."

Bob's link with Andy's first wife, Barbara, Bob's co-star in *The Lost Colony*, was clear. "Barbara would have a few cocktails and call Bob to talk about the old times," Sue said. "They had a very close relationship before and after her marriage to Andy."

Once, Sue and Bob attended a party at the home of Ainslie Pryor's widow, Pinky, in the Mandeville Canyon neighborhood of Los Angeles. Bob and Mrs. Pryor probably reminisced about the early days in *The Lost Colony*, when Bob, Andy and Ainslie bonded over their creativity and dreams.

Sue and Bob Armstrong divorced in 1976.

Susan "Sue" Guthrie Lowrance, who played a colonist and dancer during the 1978 *Lost Colony* season, with Chuck Wagner, who played John Borden that year. *Photo by J. Foster Scott, Courtesy Susan Guthrie Lowrance.*

In the summer of 1978, Sue returned to Roanoke Island to be closer to her family and rejoin *The Lost Colony* as a dancer and a colonist. Andy was still married to Cassuto, who was not on the island that summer.

Andy asked Sue to live on his estate for the summer and help him look after Dixie, who was also in the pageant. Sue agreed to do so.

———⊶∞⊷———

When she was fourteen, Dixie visited with her father as he filmed a 1974 TV movie, *Winter Kill*, in Big Bear Lake, California. The movie included an all-but-unknown Nick Nolte. Dixie waterskied with her father and Nolte. After graduating from high school in 1977, she worked on two TV pilot movies as a costume apprentice with MGM studios. "It was a wonderful time working side-by-side with Dad," Dixie said. "The camaraderie on the set was fantastic, and my dad was very proud."

Back on the island, Dixie and her father took part with island buddies in rowdy volleyball games on beaches by the Sound. Andy, as always, had to win at all costs. During one especially contentious game, he contested referee calls to the point that one teenager yelled at him, "Oh, go sit on a Ritz, Andy," a reference to a recent hokey commercial for Ritz crackers Andy had done for the money.

The game stopped, and everybody shut up, knowing the boy had gone to a forbidden spot. Andy stared a hole in him. Then he kicked the boy so hard in his rear end that he all but broke a toe.

That summer of 1978, Sue lived in the maid's room, adjacent to the kitchen.

Andy traveled back and forth to Los Angeles that summer. "One day," Sue said, "he came to my room and said he needed talk to me. He told me that he had been dreaming about me. It was an uncomfortable moment for me. I told him, 'You broke my heart in 1972. I just can't go through that again, but I will always be your friend.' That was the only time that summer that Andy and I spoke to each other about our relationship.

"I kept my boundaries as I knew in my heart that it just wasn't right to rekindle our relationship. Not only was he married to Solica, but I had married and divorced one of his closest friends. I wanted to maintain our friendship, because that was important to me."

On a return visit to the Outer Banks in the summer of 1979, Sue met Andy and friends at the Sound Side, a legendary bar in Kill Devil Hills known for good music and sunsets on the Sound. Andy had helped in getting Doc Watson, a renowned country-blues/mountain music guitarist, to play at the bar. Andy and Doc both hailed from northwestern North Carolina and were about the same age. At one point that night, Sue, Andy and others stood in the sand parking lot of the bar with a recorder Sue had brought, Andy taping a greeting to Bob Armstrong for Sue to take back to California as a surprise.

In the 1980s, Sue entered the hospitality field, going on to become a hotel sales director and an independent meeting planner. She considers herself blessed to have had a wonderful thirteen-year marriage in San Diego to a retired U.S. Navy submarine commander until his passing.

Sue and Dixie have remained friends.

6

JOINING WITH THE ISLANDERS

And that's where I feel lucky. In all, over the years of coming here...I wore them down. And they accepted me.
—Andy in the 1982 David Stick interview

*I*n the early 1970s, some of Andy's closest beach friends found a good excuse for a trip out to visit him at his California home. A Jeep stolen from Fred Murray's Auto Supply in Nags Head had been recovered in the Los Angeles area. Phone calls were exchanged with Andy, excitedly setting up the trip. Murray, Ray White and Quentin Bell and his then-wife, Lee, flew out to recover the Jeep. Andy met them at the airport in his Rolls-Royce and received them warmly for a stay at his at his Toluca Lake house.

Andy needed his beach friends as much as they needed hm. They kept him real. He had show business friends, but he was not as tight with them. He wanted to show his beach friends his slice of California.

Andy and those friends would stay close in the years to come. A few years later, when Lee Bell was being treated for cancer at a Houston hospital, Andy arranged for a jet to fly her back to the island. She died in 1979. Andy was with Quentin at the funeral. "That meant a lot," Quentin said. And when Quentin later remarried, to June Temple, Andy sang "The Wedding Song" at the ceremony, the only time he ever sang at a wedding.

Andy's Rolls-Royce in front of his California home during the visit from his beach friends. *Courtesy Quentin Bell.*

Andy with one of his antique cars as beach friends Ray White and Lee Bell visited him in California in the 1970s. *Courtesy Quentin Bell.*

Ray White with Jack "Howard Sprague" Dodson, of Andy's namesake series, during the California visit. *Courtesy Quentin Bell.*

Andy shooting pool in his California home during the visit from his beach friends. *Courtesy Quentin Bell.*

—∞∞—

Andy kept working, always trying to live up to his early promise. In 1975, he starred in the Hollywood film *Hearts of the West* with a rising Jeff Bridges, a comedy about B-movie Westerns in the 1930s. The scenes between the forty-nine-year-old Andy and Bridges are strong, Andy playing a veteran hand counseling Bridges as an actor breaking into Westerns, just as, in real life, Andy was helping the younger star along by acting with him.

Critics liked the movie. It fizzled at the box office.

In summers back on the island, Andy renewed longstanding ties with the Basnights, Harveys, Bells, Owens and other families and friends. One of the ties was with Edward Greene. Greene was a short and wiry New York City native who'd arrived on the island in 1953 to work in *The Lost Colony* as the assistant choreographer, in time for Andy's last season in the play. Just as Andy had been, Greene was blown away by the island's beauty and its nonjudgmental, welcoming nature.

In 1967, with his business partner Richard Lacerre, Greene started the Christmas Shop in Manteo, a store dedicated to celebrating the holiday. Privately, Andy said his friend Greene was crazy to start such a store on an island dependent on summer tourism. But the shop took off. Andy loved to buy gifts there for family and friends. He would call ahead to avoid tourists, and Greene and Larcerre would let him in early mornings, before they opened the shop.

In the early 1970s, Greene asked Andy to pose in a photo ad for the store's promotion of *Godspell* and *Stop the World: I Want to Get Off* at the shop's Show Place. Andy did it, saying in the ad, "This is doggone good theater and I was real impressed. The talent and youthful energy of both casts make The Show Place a must for everybody, young and old."

It was one more way Andy gave back to his island and encouraged young performers to harness their talent and chase their dreams, just as he had done there.

Greene, a leader in the island's runup to the celebration of the country's bicentennial in 1976, soon had another request for Andy. He was helping engineer a tabletop book on the Outer Banks. He asked Andy to write a foreword. The result is one of the only public pieces of writing Andy left behind, a moving and funny essay about his early days on the island. In the piece for *Reflections of the Outer Banks*, by the late Donald and Carol McAdoo, Andy gives a shoutout to Ainslie Pryor:

Today is a pretty November day and I have been out walking along the shore of my land near the north end of Roanoke Island, just looking around at the countryside and thinking about this book.... When I first came here in '47, the highway heading south ended at Whalebone Junction (where you... head towards Oregon Inlet and Hatteras.) And it's really only recently that we have conveniences such as the bridges that have brought in many thousands of people from other parts of the country. One time, some of us in The Lost Colony *took a trip to Oregon Inlet and it took all day since there was no road. The possibility of getting stuck in the sand was, let's just say, immense, and we knew we had to get back in time for the show that night. So we took two cars. We made it back—all in one car!*

There used to a wooden bridge across the Roanoke Sound and when a large boat or one with a large mast came through, the bridge tender had to crank it open manually. He would let down the barricades and then put a kind of huge key in the middle of the bridge and push it around in a big circle and that opened the bridge. It took a long time. Well, a friend of mine, Ainslie Pryor, and myself one day rented a sailboat in Wanchese and sailed her around to Manteo. When we got to the bridge, it was just about high noon on Saturday, an August day, and the beach was full. We blew our whistle and the bridge tender went about his usual duties. As I say it took a long time, and by the time he got the bridge open, we had cars backed up out of sight. You may not believe it, but then we becalmed. We must have looked silly sitting there in our bathing suits and our beards (we were both in The Lost Colony*) looking at all those cars and all those cars looking at us. Neither one of us were sailors and we didn't know what to do. We tried to push through with a pole; we kept going in circles. By now, horns were blowing and people were starting to yell. We finally figured out if Ainslie would pole and I would hold the tiller, we would go in a straight line and finally get through.*

As we passed, some man on the bridge said, "Who are those fools?" Well, it happened that our director was stranded on the bridge with everybody else and he said, "That's Sir Walter Raleigh and Governor White making their last voyage."

The book, with fine vignettes of locals by Carol McAdoo and dreamy paintings and sketches of Andy and others by Carol's husband, Bob, is treasured by many Outer Bankers and their visitors, especially because of those words from Andy.

Andy always had a soft spot for local grocery stores. He had worked in one while he was in school back in Mount Airy. In two episodes of the AG show, Opie works in the Mayberry grocery store.

In 1958, Andy's buddy Chesley Midgett Jr. bought the store where he worked in downtown Manteo. Twenty years later, Chesley and his wife, Ruby, moved the store to Highway 64 in Manteo, where it could hook into the heavy tourist traffic.

When the new Food-A-Rama opened in Manteo on a hot day in 1978, Andy spoke at the event. The Manteo High School band played. One of the band members was Claudia Fry (now Claudia Fry Sluder Harrington). Claudia was a playmate of Andy's children when they were all little. Andy nicknamed her "Claude." At the grocery store opening, Claudia, who had run around to get in place before being tapped for a solo trumpet performance, played "Feelings," a hit pop song of the time. As she finished perfectly, she fainted due to the heat. Andy, long-limbed, loose and natural in a sport coat, deadpanned for the crowd, evoking laughs: "Well, there goes Claude."

Louise Overman, who worked at Food-A-Rama's downtown location as a teenager, remembered Andy coming in, often buying limes for his vodka tonics. Locals say they knew when Andy was cruising the Sound in his pontoon boat by the trail of lime rinds bobbing in his wake.

7

ANDY'S POLITICAL AWAKENING

I tried to stay out of any public life down here for a very long time. I never wanted to make any money off this place…because I felt I could get along a lot better with people if I just made my living doing what I do. And I didn't get involved in their politics.
—Andy in the David Stick interview

*I*n the late 1970s, Andy cautiously entered island politics. His concern was a land-use plan that threatened to bring commercial development to his northern end of the island, near his estate and that of his beloved Waterside Theater.

The town of Manteo's plan embraced preservation, but Andy's property was outside the town limits, in Dare County. County commissioners leaned toward development on the North End. Manteo mayor John Wilson enlisted the brilliant Professor Randy Hester and graduate students from the N.C. State University School of Design to write the town's land-use plan, and Andy had followed that process. The big challenge was to persuade Dare County commissioners to back off development and embrace a similar plan.

Andy learned how to work the political levers, back-channel, reaching out to friends and acquaintances, quickly finding out who would help him and who would not.

He told David Stick: "While it frightened me to death, and, I, having never done it before, I went out on a one-on-one campaign to stop that [development] from happening." He telephoned, visited with and wrote letters to those connected to the issue and to Dare County commissioners. "I started to get people behind it," Andy said. "I'm talking about other citizens in town.…Because I had, by now, I started to gain momentum. When I first

Left: Andy's first wife, Barbara (*far left*), on a cruise in the 1970s with her good beach friend Elsie May Bell (*center*), the mother of his goddaughter Bea. *Courtesy Bea Bell.*

Below: Andy at Elsie May's wake. *Courtesy Bea Bell.*

started talking to people, I didn't do very well because I didn't know how. But then, as I started to sell myself on this North End, I started to do better and I started to really work at it."

Andy and his friends won in persuading the commissioners to adopt a land-use plan that kept most commercial development off the North End.

One of Andy's closest friends said: "Andy came out full force in the end, lobbied like a pro."

Andy compared the feeling he got from that first political victory to his show business wins. "It's different, but it's alike at the same time," he told Stick. "The adrenaline is really going crazy."

His political emergence came with tension.

"There are people who are going to resent," Andy told Stick. "Then there is a mentality that is going to resent success. You know that. When I was poor in Mount Airy, all my people resented people who had success and money. It's just natural to do: If you ain't got it, hate them that's got it. Well, I got this silly looking pontoon boat that I go around in, people see it, they know it's mine, and they think it's silly....But I have a wonderful time in it.

"And I know that some of them say it's stupid, he's probably a fag, he's running around with these young women, what the hell's the matter with him, something's wrong, something's got to be wrong. So there is a mentality that's gonna do that. However, there is another mentality that is deeply appreciative that people like you and I will spend our energy working for what we believe to be the good of the whole community."

Andy continued to be there for the beach friends from his days with Barbara. His friend John Bell had died years before, and John's widow, Elsie May, had remained close to Barbara.

In the summer of 1980, Barbara was dying in a California hospital of breast cancer that had spread to her brain. Dixie visited her daily. At one point, Andy told Dixie: "I think I need to go see your mother." Dixie said, "I think he just needed to make peace. He loved her dearly for many years."

Andy went to Barbara's room, just the two of them. He told Dixie he was glad he visited. Barbara, in that late stage, asked Dixie, "Who was that man? He was very nice."

Barbara died on July 23, 1980. She was just fifty-three.

Elsie May died just over a year later, in August 1981, of kidney failure. Andy stopped by Twiford's Funeral Home in Manteo, hands tucked awkwardly in the pockets of his tan suit, trying to find the right words to say when no words would do, just as Sheriff Taylor might have done.

A few years later, Dare County sheriff Bert Austin rode by Andy walking toward another funeral in downtown Manteo. Austin stopped and asked his friend if he needed a ride. Andy thanked him but said he needed to be "with the people," Austin remembered.

8

A COMMUNITY FOUNDATION AND A PARTY CELEBRATING THE ISLAND

Why does a nationally known actor, still active in a career that calls for him to spend most of his time in Hollywood, California, consider Roanoke Island, North Carolina, his home?
—Outer Banks author David Stick's question to Andy,
setting up the June 1982 interview

On June 8, 1982, Andy sat down with David Stick for a long interview at Stick's home in the town of Southern Shores on the northern Outer Banks, a drive of almost an hour in the summer traffic from Andy's island home. Stick's father, Frank, had been an accomplished artist and pioneer real-estate man on the Banks in a good way, a leading force om preserving federal land on Hatteras Island, then carefully developing Southern Shores. David Stick had done well in real estate himself, also balancing that with conservation and preservation. He was the premier chronicler of Banks history through several books.

Stick and Andy sat at a round table in Stick's study, two friends talking. Stick cut on a tape recorder. Andy had just turned fifty-six seven days before. His was friendly, easy and sophisticated, with only a mild Southern drawl. He was surprisingly open, especially in talking about his hometown: "I can drive up to Mount Airy right now and get a hot spot in the middle of my chest that will not leave until I get out of there."

Andy talked of another island. Once, he said, he and his second and now ex-wife, Solica, had gone to Maui, Hawaii. "I had one day that I had fun on the Big Island," Andy told Stick. "A fellow, a veterinarian that I met over there, took me on a hunting trip above the tree-line. I didn't enjoy the hunting, but [did] enjoy the landscape....But I remember staying at this place on Maui and taking those little beach chairs and your oil and your magazine and going out there and sitting with these other people from the Midwest and places. I remember going out there and sitting down. I was with Solica. Dick [Linke] had given us that trip as a wedding present....

"This was at a hotel. Go out by the pool there and sit in these little chairs. I sat there maybe 20 minutes reading and looking around. Finally, I thought, 'What are we doing here?' She said, 'I don't know.' I said, 'Well, let's go.' So we did, went in and checked out, got on an airplane, and as soon as I could after that I came out here."

Lee Greenway, his longtime makeup man, would occasionally visit Roanoke Island to hunt with Andy and his friends.

Once, Andy visited Greenway at his home in Rutherfordton, in Western North Carolina, not that far from Andy's foothills hometown. As they rode around Rutherfordton one day, Andy told his friend, "Lee, I've got to tell you something. It's beautiful up here, but it doesn't make me feel comfortable." Andy elaborated: "'Cause you carry a feeling, you know?"

That feeling was his love for Roanoke Island.

"I've been trying, for a while now, to get back to work," he told Stick. "You tend to, when you go for long periods without working, you tend to start doubting yourself. And you tend to start wondering, 'How do you do those things?' They come back automatically. But, uh, thank God they do."

He was continuing to test himself, adjusting to playing older characters in TV movies with rising stars, having just the year before acted in *Murder in Texas* with Farrah Fawcett and Sam Elliott.

Andy talked about self-doubt: "Everybody has that, isn't that interesting? Will Rogers never thought his career would last...and nobody, most people that I have ever come in contact with, believe[s] they're going to survive beyond what they're doing right that minute, unless they've got these gigantic egos, and some do."

As Andy said those lines, it might have occurred to them that Rogers, the blue-collar, or blue-bandana, Western comedian was one of the models for Andy's Dusty Rhodes in *A Face in the Crowd*, because Rogers reportedly, in private, ridiculed his working-class fans.

Andy talked about his old friend Don Knotts. He said he'd told Dick Linke that "I'd love to do something with Don. He's contacting CBS to see if he can put something together with Don. I don't know whether we can or not. Don and I had a certain magic at one time. Whether we can re-create that or not, I don't know."

After the interview ended, Stick and Andy talked on for a bit. Andy said he was grateful to the island for giving him his start. "Sometime, I'd like to find some way to pay them back," he said. Stick said he had recently learned about the concept of community foundations, which had begun to take root in other parts of the country in the early 1900s. They agreed a foundation might be a fine way to give back. "Let's go with it," Andy said.

A few weeks later, Stick called Andy's *Lost Colony* alum buddy Edward Greene and Nags Head businessman George Crocker and asked them to meet at Crocker's Nags Head house on a topic to be revealed. Stick could be dramatic, in his own dry way. He had let Andy in on the secret, that the subject would be starting a local community foundation, but kept in the dark their friends Greene and Crocker, who exchanged phone calls, trying to figure out the mystery.

Crocker was a legend in his own right. A Virginia Beach native, he hit the Outer Banks in 1953 with a sixth-grade education, a $15,000 loan and a dream of being an entrepreneur, Wayne and Nancy Beach Gray wrote

Andy with friends during the initial planning of the Outer Banks Community Foundation in the summer of 1982. Andy (*left to right*), David Stick, Edward Greene and George Crocker. *Photo by Walter V. Gresham III.*

in *Legendary Locals of the Northern Outer Banks*. George launched the Galleon Esplanade store, the Cabana East and Beacon motels, a namesake restaurant and an antique car museum. He did it all with his own flamboyant, innovative style. Then he gave back in ways that included a Manteo High School scholarship. Through it all, he had fun, laughing and telling stories. He was gay and beloved on the nonjudgmental Banks. Andy bought some of his clothes from the men's shop at Crocker's Galleon, knowing George was forged by talent, hard work and Banks magic, just as he was.

At Crocker's house, the men sipped coffee as Stick unveiled his plan: A community foundation for the Outer Banks to help its residents in myriad ways, from scholarship funds to losses wrought by hurricanes. The men embraced the plan.

The core group soon grew to include Andy's old friend banker Ray White; attorney Martin Kellogg; and accountant Jack Adams. They crafted their founding documents and recruited a board of directors, with Andy serving as the figurehead to attract attention to their cause. At a press conference in November 1982, they announced the creation of the Outer Banks Community Foundation, meeting with widespread support. The foundation soon had contributions of more than $90,000 and made an initial award of $10,000 in grants to local nonprofits.

Andy's next step in giving back was taking part in North Carolina's plans for the country's 400th anniversary and, coupled with it, the revitalization of downtown Manteo. The plans began in 1982 and included the building of the *Elizabeth II*, a representative of the ship in which the colonists who would be lost in 1587 arrived, culminating with the celebration in 1987. "Andy didn't want to become involved," one of his close island friends said, "but he became very involved":

> *Governor Jim Hunt asked him to serve on America's 400th Anniversary Committee. Hunt and* [soon-to-be state senator Marc] *Basnight asked me if I thought he would serve. I said "maybe," really doubting he would. But I thought his name would be beneficial to the celebration, and helpful in raising the money for the* Elizabeth II. *I did not think he could bear to sit through those all-day, boring meetings. But after Hunt appointed him, he became way more involved than I ever thought he would. We drove*

to the meetings together; he came from California just because we had a meeting. He was sincerely honored to have been appointed by the governor and he took it seriously.

Andy worked closely with his friends John Wilson, the Manteo mayor, and Edward Greene, who was on the Manteo town board, on the general effort. Andy insisted that events leading up to the date had to be festive, a big party. The island had to look good for that. The revitalization of downtown Manteo and landscaping of the entrance to the island from the mainland bridge was a big part of that. Billboards and trash lined that corridor. Downtown was sagging, with many businesses having left for the busy beach.

Breaking his carefully constructed privacy, Andy, in 1982, gave Hunt a well-publicized tour of downtown Manteo, walking past the beat-down buildings and sagging docks and pointing out all it needed.

Hunt brought in the money for the effort. Town officials secured federal funds as well. On the corridor, the billboards and trash were taken out and trees were planted. There was a fun series of events, just as Andy had wanted, drawing in celebrities ranging from English royalty to legendary TV anchorman Walter Cronkite, a waterman in his own right, a yachtsman. Hunt said in 2020 that Andy was an important part of the planning, and "the island was lucky to have him."

It all sprang from Andy's love of that spot of sand. "Mount Airy is where I wanted to escape from, and Manteo is where I escaped to. I fell in love with the classless society I found among the cast of *The Lost Colony*," he told his local friend Angel Ellis Khoury for her 1999 book *Manteo: A Roanoke Island Town*.

Andy kept giving back to the pageant, making commercials for it and, best of all, pulling his boat up for impromptu visits with the crew and popping into occasional scenes before the live audience, veteran *Colony* hands David Miller and Gail Hutchison recalled.

"He'd often 'appear' backstage and pick up a hat and cape from the costume area," said Hutchison, who took on several crew and cast roles, including time as Agona, off and on, from 1981 to 1993. "As an actor/tech and then assistant stage manager, I'd see him get ready, then enter the stage for a crowd scene with such delight. He'd blend right in, ad lib a line, and then the crew would know he was there. Other times, we would see him in his pontoon boat, floating by the backstage and giving us a wave."

Manteo mayor John Wilson, Governor Jim Hunt and Andy walk the beat-down streets of downtown Manteo during the push for revitalization in 1982. *William Parker photo, Outer Banks History Center, State Archives of North Carolina.*

Andy continued to search for challenging film roles. In 1985, he played a gay cattle baron in the Western spoof *Rustlers' Rhapsody*. Some critics praised Andy's work, but the film got nowhere at the box office.

Mayberry kept calling. In 1986, NBC came out with the TV film *Return to Mayberry*, reuniting Andy, Don Knotts and many of the other stars from the show. Ron Howard, by then in his early thirties, told the author he had some trepidation going into it. As the AG show ended when he was in his early teens, he remembered Andy and the rest of the cast treating him as a peer. "I wondered if these people could possibly live up to my recollections," Howard said. "In a very honest way, they did." He talked with Andy off-screen during the 1986 show. "I just recognized how thoughtful he was about everything he did," Howard said. "He was very measured about his career."

9

MATLOCK BRINGS IT HOME

In bringing Matlock to the island and so many other ways,
Andy always looked out for the locals.
—*Bert Austin, Dare County sheriff, 1982–2002*

The islanders had been there for Andy in his tough times. He'd make damn sure they'd be with him in his good times. As he made his career comeback as Atlanta lawyer Ben Matlock in the popular *Matlock* TV series, Andy brought the show from its Los Angeles filming site to Manteo for a double episode in the summer of 1989.

He told a reporter that Manteo was "very meaningful" to him, Terry Collins notes in his book *The Andy Griffith Story*. "This is where I became an entertainer."

The episode was one more step in his repaying his debt to the island, reaching out to the friends who had helped launch his career four decades ago.

"He wanted to pay back a lot of people he loved," Della Basnight said. "He wanted to show Manteo off and he wanted very much for his *Matlock* family to know the town. Andy really did love everybody. There are so many people who had their own personal relationships or encounters with Andy."

Some critics had written him off, but now he had another prime-time hit, twenty years after the AG show had ended. Few in American show biz came back like that in their sixties, especially after significant physical problems like Andy had experienced. He had compounded the childhood injury to

Above: Filming of the *Matlock* episode in front of the courthouse in downtown Manteo in 1989. *Photo by Drew C. Wilson via the Outer Banks History Center, State Archives.*

Left: Andy during the filming of "The Hunting Party." *Drew C. Wilson photo, Outer Banks History Center, State Archives of North Carolina.*

his back by falling off a ladder while working on the roof at his Toluca Lake house. As he started filming *Matlock*, he wore knee braces because of a recent bout with Guillain-Barré syndrome, a rare form of nerve inflammation that can cripple. The braces had stopped him from going barefoot on his island, which must have emotionally hurt Andy.

But locals said he was a bear at barreling through physical challenges, rarely talking about them. He had learned resilience from his fellow islanders, including commercial fishermen his age who were still building boats and manning them. His third wife, Cindi, a *Lost Colony* actress whom he'd met through the pageant and married in 1983, loyally backed him.

Matlock, which ran from 1986 to 1995, was not art, but it was entertaining, popular and made good money. Andy had Don Knotts in for several guest roles, as well as Aneta Corsaut, who would die just a few years later of cancer at the at the age of sixty-two, playing a judge.

Andy helped his friends out by giving them those parts, just as he aided others, sometimes finding them serendipitously, such as Brownie McGhee, a blues musician he had long admired. McGhee had coached Andy on his guitar playing in *Face in the Crowd*. One summer in the late 1980s, Andy was in his friend Jack Sandberg's Yellowhouse Galleries in Nags Head when Andy heard Brownie singing on a CD Jack's framer, Tom Tully, was playing. Sandberg remembered:

> *Andy recognized Brownie's voice immediately and proceeded to tell us how he had met him on the set of* Face in the Crowd. *Andy remembered him fondly. He told us a lot about making that movie for Elia Kazan, and then wondered what might have happened to Brownie in the ensuing 30 years. He said that, after he returned to California, he was going to try to locate Brownie and get back in touch. Much to our surprise, a year or so later (On May 9, 1989 to be precise) an episode of* Matlock *appeared, titled* The Blues Singer, *in which Matlock defends a musician who has been falsely accused of murder. Brownie* [age seventy-three] *appeared briefly in that episode as a friend of the defendant. Andy had not only located Brownie, still performing occasionally in the Oakland area, but had a whole show written around him, and brought him down to Hollywood to appear in it, greatly improving Brownie's late-career financial position in the process.*

Andy continued to stay involved in island civic matters. A typewritten letter he dictated in March 1989 to a Manteo friend bore the letterhead of "Law Offices, Benjamin L. Matlock." Andy, probably winking, added a P.S.: "I apologize for the stationery, but it is the fastest way I could get the letter out."

As he thought about the best way to bring his show to Manteo, Andy, who had major say on scripts, toyed with a couple of story ideas. One would have been loosely based on a 1967 murder on the island, that of Brenda Joyce Holland, the nineteen-year-old makeup supervisor at *The Lost Colony*, whose body was found in the Sound after a massive search. She had been strangled and may have been raped. The murder remained unsolved, a black eye to local and state law enforcement agents.

Another case Andy considered was that of Cloice Creef, a former caretaker for the courthouse whose body was found by the roadside in 1979 near the gate to Andy's house. Two prominent citizens were convicted in connection with a hit-and-run. Some locals contended Creef had been killed before the car hit him, his body thrown in front of the car to protect the real killer, who'd allegedly been battling Creef over a woman who lived nearby.

Ultimately, local friends talked an initially obstinate Andy out of fictionalizing either story, telling him the controversy would not be worth it. Andy led in a script that came to be called "The Hunting Party." It concerns a murder, rare for the island, and drug smuggling, not rare for the island or the rest of the Outer Banks. In the 1980s, smugglers, modern-day pirates, were using the hundreds of desolate canals on the Banks and surrounding areas to boat in pot and cocaine to be loaded into cars and trucks. Often, authorities closed in on the boats bringing in the drugs. Sometimes, the crews

Andy with his *Lost Colony* buddy R.G. "Bob" Armstrong in 1979 on the set of Andy's short-lived TV series *Salvage*. Bob was there for a guest appearance as a sheriff. The duo looked much the same in costume ten years later when they appeared together in "The Hunting Party" episode of *Matlock. Floyd "Chunk" Simmons photo, Outer Banks History Center, State Archives of North Carolina.*

Andy talks with Bob Armstrong, playing the local sheriff, during the filming of "The Hunting Party." *Courtesy Ken Mann.*

dumped their contents in the Gulf Stream before they could be busted. A popular local T-shirt showed a bale of pot floating near a boat with the logo "Save the Bales," a take on the "Save the Whales" slogan. The floating bales were tempting for commercial fisherman and charter boat captains, who often faced financial hardship. One local charter boat captain scooped up a bale, then told his fellow "cappies" over the maritime radio that he had harvested it and his financial problems were solved. Legal problems ensued, but the captain somehow beat them.

Andy would have heard such stories as he gave input to the writers on "The Hunting Party." He labored over the script, scribbling in numerous changes, ones to make it flow more freely, using local names such as "Mother Vineyard" to ensure it would sound authentic to the critics he valued most, his fellow islanders.

Andy had a sure feel for local law enforcement. He was friends with Dare County sheriff Bert Austin, who served as a technical adviser on "The Hunting Party." Andy had endorsed Austin in his political campaigns and often stopped by the sheriff's office, in the old courthouse in downtown Manteo, to chat. As the North Carolina Sheriffs' Association prepared to hold its annual meeting one year at a Kill Devil Hills hotel, Austin asked

Andy to give a speech. Andy agreed to do so. Austin put out the word Andy would be speaking, leading to record attendance for the event. Andy rendered wonderful words about playing Sheriff Taylor and teared up as he talked about Don Knotts and, surprisingly, Frances Bavier (Aunt Bee), whom he respected as an actress but did not have fun with offstage. Austin also asked Andy to speak at a national convention of sheriffs in Nashville. Once again, Andy came through for his friend, charming the crowd.

For "The Hunting Party," Andy brought in Bob Armstrong, making his first visit back since his *Lost Colony* days, to play the local sheriff. They were together again on the island that launched their dreams.

Andy carefully included many locals in "The Hunting Party." He enlisted friends including Marjalene Thomas, her son Hunt, Quentin and June Bell and others to play as extras, including some members of that year's *Lost Colony* cast.

Andy also recruited Cora Mae Basnight, who'd become an icon for her side-splitting role as Agona in *The Lost Colony*. Just as Andy was for other island friends, he'd always been there for Cora Mae. When Cora Mae's ex-husband died, Andy realized she might be feeling lonely on the day of the funeral. He drove up to her house in Manteo on Agona Street, named for her *Lost Colony* character, and found Cora Mae sitting alone on her porch. Andy took a seat beside her, saying, "Cora Mae, let's talk about the good times." She loved it, welcoming her old friend. It was vintage Andy, the best of the man himself and the sheriff he'd played on TV.

Cora Mae initially resisted being in "The Hunting Party." Andy visited with her on her front porch once again, charming her into taking part.

Craig Fincannon, the location casting director on the island shoot, said, "Andy is such an enigma, even to those who were around him." There was the man, and there

Another shot of Andy during the filming of "The Hunting Party." *Drew C. Wilson photo, Outer Banks History Center, State Archives of North Carolina.*

Cora Mae Basnight, Andy and an unidentified friend on Cora Mae's front porch in Manteo during the filming of "The Hunting Party" in 1989. *Courtesy Claudia Fly Sluder Harrington.*

was the Sheriff Taylor tag. "That is a heavy burden, you know, that can be a heavy cross to bear," Fincannon said. "Andy was so personally 'Mr. North Carolina.' Everybody in this state felt he was their daddy or brother or old boyfriend. The fact that he didn't fall down the rabbit hole of Hollywood stardom says a lot about him." Compared to some of today's actors, Fincannon said, Andy's off-screen life was tame.

As always, Andy the perfectionist had to get it right. At times, Fincannon said, Andy "would dress down an assistant director and look to the other side and wink at somebody else. It was a defense mechanism."

Near the start of the episode, Della Basnight plays a local spotting Matlock arriving at the courthouse, saying, "That's him!"

Andy was not satisfied. "Don't do it like that," he said in front of the crowd. He told Della he wanted her to announce Matlock's arrival in a lower voice. She did so, and Andy said, "That's fine."

Andy had shots of local businesses dropped in. In one scene, *Outer Banks Magazine*, the publication of his friend Angel Ellis Khoury, is on the bedside table of Matlock's motel room.

The author Nancy Beach Gray remembers the crew filming a scene at the Wanchese restaurant she and her late husband, Wayne, owned, the *Queen Anne's Revenge*:

It was like the circus came to town when they rolled up with trailer after trailer pulled by Mac trucks and well over 75 people! They even had their own food truck. Andy stayed in his own air-conditioned caravan until they needed him on camera. He came out and did his thing, and then went right back in. He was dressed in his signature seersucker Matlock suit. At one point, everything stopped as he went to get a haircut with a barber that they brought along.

The production team was very gracious. We weren't expecting any money, but they insisted on paying us. Finally, Wayne and my dad said, "How about $250.00 for our employee Christmas party?" They cut a check on the spot. When the show finally came out, even though the outdoor setting was unrecognizable to most Queen Anne's fans, they panned our sign as the segment began. I thought that was kind of them.

Toward the end of the shooting, Laura Bostwick, a bedrock islander, hosted a dinner party for Bob Armstrong and other key cast and crew members, and key locals such as Della Basnight, at Bostwick's Wanchese home. It was wild and glorious fun. Andy did not attend, opting to save

Andy with former Manteo mayor John Wilson, his longtime friend, during the final scene of "The Hunting Party." *Drew C. Wilson photo, Outer Banks History Center, State Archives of North Carolina.*

Andy during the final scene of "The Hunting Party" with Cora Mae Basnight and many other island friends. *Drew C. Wilson photo.*

his energy. He was only sixty-two, but coming back from Guillain-Barré syndrome had taxed him.

In a courtroom scene the next day, the partygoers of the night before made a few mistakes. During a break in the shooting, Andy confronted Bob, only half-jokingly, in front of all: "Did you go out with Della Basnight last night? I told you not to run with her, she'll kill you.'"

In the last scene, Andy's Matlock stands in front of the courthouse in downtown Manteo, greeting his real-life island friends. There were members of the Owens and Basnight families, closely tied through marriage, and most of all, Cora Mae Basnight. One cameraman joked that a T-shirt should say "If you ain't a Basnight in this town, you ain't s———"

"'The Hunting Party,'" Fincannon said, was "a sort of gigantic family reunion."

In 1993, Andy persuaded his producers to bring the full-time filming of *Matlock* from Los Angeles to Wilmington, North Carolina. Or to put it bluntly, he just told them: "That's it, I'm going to North Carolina." *Matlock*, a show set in Atlanta that was filmed in Los Angeles, would now be shot in North Carolina.

Andy's push was personal: He wanted to be able to plane-commute to his Roanoke Island house, finally making it his full-time home. But he also knew it would help his state's burgeoning film industry, of which Wilmington was the bedrock.

Bill Vassar, head of the EUE/Screen Gems studio complex in Wilmington, told the *Star-News* of Wilmington that *Matlock* helped pave the way for other series, notably *Dawson's Creek* and *One Tree Hill*, to pick southeastern North Carolina as a location. "That's what kept the film industry going here," he said.

Andy commuted to the set from his Manteo home, a pilot flying him in on a small plane, living in Wilmington during the week. He worked hard and wrapped Friday afternoons, hopping on the plane and pouring white wine into a plastic cup for the flight home.

In Wilmington while filming *Matlock*, Andy walked freely around town, said Fincannon, who continued there as location casting director. "He didn't have bodyguards; he didn't have a posse. He made himself vulnerable. He had long since learned how a stare or an attitude could protect hm, just to give him some breathing room."

Andy, Fincannon said, was always professional on the stage set. "It was hard work for him. He never used cue cards. He did it old school, captured it in one or two takes, and then he was out on Friday afternoon to get back to Manteo."

Chester Spier, the property master on the set, agreed. "Andy was more than a professional," he said. "He was amazing." He said Andy was often jovial off camera, once asking him and others what doctors did with the penis after a sex-change operation. "He was ribbing the guys…that was just his way of having fun in a nice way, not in a mean way."

Spier, who is gay, said Andy was supportive of his marriage to his partner: "Andy had a lot of friends who were gay. He was just very much for civil rights, for equality for everybody. He didn't make a big point of it. He was just supportive of people being themselves." Spier said Andy told him he left a church because the minister preached a sermon against gay marriage.

Andy quietly supported Wilmington charities, Spier said, including making sure a police drive to supply toys for poor children at Christmas met its goal—on the condition he stayed in the background. "He would make up the difference to make sure every kid had a toy," Spier said.

Jeff Loy, an Outer Banks native who worked on the Wilmington set as a grip and rigger, said that Andy ran such a smooth set that the slogan was "I've died and gone to *Matlock*." Loy remembered Griffith speaking to his class at Kitty Hawk Elementary School in the early 1970s. "We all knew it was kind of cool," Loy said.

Loy's father ran Cap'n Dave's Restaurant in Kill Devil Hills. Loy, as a teenager, waited on Andy there. Andy treated him fine, Loy said, but there was a certain tension. "You're always tensed for the waiter to say something or do something that treats him differently, that might make him feel uncomfortable."

When Loy first started working on the set, he and Andy would briefly chat. But once Andy realized Loy was from his home sand, Andy no longer sought him out. Loy didn't mind, saying "One of the things that dawned on me working with him on *Matlock* and being around that all whole environment: You got to understand that there's not a person on the friggin' planet that doesn't know who Andy Griffith is. Especially as he got older: He'd be thinking: 'I'm tired, I'm doing my job, and everybody wants a piece of me.'"

Andy couldn't wait to get back to his island on weekends. His close local friends were his people, the ones in whom he confided. Andy's son, Sam, died in 1996 after years of drug and alcohol abuse. Andy and Sam had been estranged. Andy talked to his island confidants of his regrets about not being able to save Sam. Andy told Dixie that he chose not to go to Sam's funeral because his presence would have drawn out even more press photographers, disrupting the service. Dixie attended the funeral that January and said, "Sure enough, photographers with big lens cameras loomed all about."

10

ANDY TAKES ON "THE LION"

I came here a half-century ago to be in The Lost Colony. *It was a magical place then and there has been a lot of changes since, many of them good, but this Food Lion business is overkill.*
—*Andy speaking before the Manteo Board of Commissioners on April 4, 2001.*

Those principles of communities coming together meant a lot to him.
—*Ron Howard speaking of Andy's work on the AG show in a January 10, 2021 interview with the author*

*I*t was Andy Griffith channeling Sheriff Taylor, standing up for his underdog buddies against a push by top dogs, even if Citizen Andy had become a big dog in his own right. He was a visionary, gently guiding his fellow islanders past immediate economic concerns to remember their past and meld it with their future, realizing that the years ahead depended on the island's own special brand of tourism, one free from the big business-clogged mess that was happening up the beach.

In 2001, Andy spent hours resisting a push by the Food Lion grocery store chain to come to his island. He loved shopping for his tonic water, limes and other items at the Manteo Food-A-Rama run by his good friends, and he realized that the chain store would likely put them out of business. His buddy Chesley Midgett had started Food-A-Rama, and Andy had presided over the opening of its new location on U.S. 64 back in 1978. The older Andy got, the more he guarded his privacy. But even more than that, he valued loyalty. He repaid it to those who'd been loyal to him, even at the cost of his privacy, for the love of his island.

Food Lion wanted to build a store of almost forty-six-thousand square feet in Manteo and had won the tacit approval of a narrow majority of town commissioners. Andy fought back hard. "He knew what would come with it—overdevelopment and the loss of the small-town feel," said Bert Austin, who was the Dare County sheriff at the time.

It was a classic fight, David (Andy) against Goliath (Food Lion), that would underscore all the drama long existing among the islanders, fit for an AG show save for its modern overtones. At one point, a Food Lion supporter would claim in a public meeting that she had received death threats for her stance and another supporter of the chain store would claim that a local grocery continued to employ a man who masturbated in a back room.

As the battle began, Andy called Al Norman, a Massachusetts author who'd beaten back Walmart stores, to speak out against Food Lion's push, and left him a voicemail: "Al, this is Andy Griffith calling from Manteo. I wanted to talk to you about a fight were having down here with Food Lion."

Norman, who grew up watching the AG show and was also a fan of *A Face in the Crowd*, was thrilled to hear the voicemail and saved it for years. "He was taking his time to let me know it was important to him," Norman said in 2021. "I was not about to ignore somebody I thought was a pretty iconic figure in small-town America. I couldn't believe it, that someone who had created that myth, that legend of the importance of small towns, was actually on my side and needed my help. I was very honored."

Norman called Andy back and was soon involved in the Manteo fight.

⤜✸⤏

In a 2001 blog post, Norman wrote:

> *The* [proposed Food Lion] *store would have to be raised by 6 feet of fill dirt just to meet code. It's not as if Manteo shoppers have been deprived of grocery stores. They have 3 local grocers already, and addicted shoppers have Food Lions within a short drive of Manteo. There are 449 Food Lions in North Carolina alone.*

Norman spoke at a public forum at the Pioneer Theater in downtown Manteo, where Andy had presided at the local premiere of *A Face in the*

Crowd back in 1957. Protesters, mostly anti–Food Lion ones with homemade signs, packed the sidewalk outside the theater. Inside, it was crowded, due to advance word that Andy would introduce Norman. Andy took the stage, telling the audience that Norman knew his stuff, alluding to Norman's work (Andy had obviously studied it) and how that tied into the preservation of small-town America and his love of the island. Andy revved up the crowd. As Norman began his PowerPoint presentation, he told the audience, which was clapping and yelling and cheering, that Andy's introduction was a high point of his life.

Norman had been involved in similar fights nationwide, some of which he'd lost, but he began to feel that Andy's involvement would win the Manteo one. "He was a very heartfelt man," Norman said in 2021. "You could tell he meant what he said. He was really a strong presence."

⎯⎯ ⚬⚬⚬ ⎯⎯

That event was soon followed, on April 4, 2001, with Andy and several friends speaking against the Food Lion push before a regular meeting of the Manteo Board of Commissioners. Andy, after patiently waiting his place in line, was the fifth to speak:

> *I came here a half-century ago to be in* The Lost Colony. *It was a magical place then and there and there has been a lot of changes since, many of them good, but this Food Lion business is overkill, it's bad for the environment and bad for the island....If you want a Food Lion, there is one already up the beach....I love Roanoke Island and still think it's a unique and magical place. Do right by the town and vote no.*

He said that when he first came to the island, it was a bit longer and wider, but he had just learned that it was now ten miles long and two miles wide and "very fragile." His words invoking the old days, including the local phrase of "up the beach" to refer to the northern beaches, resonated with the audience. He wisely ended his remarks after just a few minutes, allowing his fellow locals, many of them his friends, including Edward Greene, to have their say, most of them speaking against Food Lion.

Next up was a May 2, 2001 public hearing. The vote on a zoning issue on whether to allow Food Lion would follow. Town officials, anticipating a big crowd, held the hearing at Manteo Middle School, instead of Town Hall.

On April 4, 2001, Andy spoke before the Manteo Board of Commissioners during the push to keep Food Lion out of Manteo. *Drew C. Wilson photo.*

The middle school, a brick building on Highway 64 that had been the high school, was the largest venue on the island.

It's fair to say that some, if not many, of those who turned out that Wednesday had heard Andy would be speaking and came just to see him. Andy knew that, happy to lend his iconic visage to a cause in which he believed. The older he got, the more his craggy features looked like they had been sculpted from Pilot Mountain near his hometown, "Mount Pilot" in the AG show. The auditorium had seating for nearly 340. With extra chairs and standing at the rear, it could hold 400. Andy had packed the room to overcapacity when he delivered the graduation speech to the class of 1970, attracting so many tourists that many family members of the graduates had to stand outside. He had talked to the graduates about pursuing alternatives, about how he was not good at studies or sports but had learned to play the trombone; then, after being told he couldn't sing, he had found his way in comedy and then into acting and how Elia Kazan had taught him how to act.

Thirty-one years later, the room was at standing-room-only capacity once more. Andy was the twenty-second person to speak in the line of sixty-four of his fellow citizens, patiently waiting his turn. He walked slowly to the podium and raised himself up to his full six feet, silver-haired

Before a standing-room-only crowd at the Manteo Middle School on May 2, 2001, Andy waited in line to make his final push against the Food Lion in Manteo. *Drew C. Wilson photo.*

and smiling, seventy-four years of life etched across his face. He knew many in the crowd, old friends and new ones. He began steadily speaking in the tenor-baritone voice he'd honed as Sir Walter Raleigh a half century before, back when he'd fallen in love with the sand sliver surrounded by that wonderous water. The room went still, spellbound by the old star whose presence with them showed he was first and foremost an islander.

He asked the commissioners seated at the stage in front of him to save the island from urban sprawl and said the chain would eliminate competition. "The size of this Food Lion is larger than the existing Food Lions and all they want to do is make money for their corporation. Remember: The island is only ten miles long and three miles wide," he said, alluding to the contention he had made at the April 4 meeting that the island once been longer and wider. Andy was on a roll, and the crowd loved him. He was one of them forever.

The Food Lion opponents waited nervously as the board dealt with other items before voting. At the last minute, one commissioner who had been for Food Lion changed his mind. His crucial swing vote sealed the defeat of the zoning amendment Food Lion needed to build the store. The commissioner who'd shifted, shocking all, abruptly left the stage and was not seen for several days thereafter.

Norman said in 2021: "It was one thing for Andy to call me in, but he was right there in the front of the fight. I could understand why Andy, who could have lived in so many places, wanted to be there."

In his blog post, Al Norman wrote:

> *Aunt Bee reminds Sheriff Andy Taylor that "politics begins at home." Viewed from the outside, the slaying of the Lion in Manteo may only seem like a small victory in a small hometown. But Manteo is much larger than it looks. It is, after all, Mayberry—a place and a lifestyle longed for by millions of Americans. All across the country, one Mayberry after another is being ravaged by developers. Home-grown activists wrestled the lion in Mayberry, and the message to developers everywhere is that if you roar at us—we're prepared to roar back!*

Food Lion wasn't done. And neither was Andy.

Food Lion, already established on the nearby beach, won rights to establish another store in Nags Head, in the same shopping center as another beloved local grocery of Andy's, Seamark Foods. Tim and Susie Walters had started Seamark in 1989. Tim Walters remembered the first time he met Andy:

> *I knew he had an account, but I hadn't seen him yet. One day, as I was bagging groceries, I heard a man say "I have a charge account." I said, before I looked up, "Who are you?" He said, "I'm the husband of Cindi Griffith." That's how I was introduced to Andy. He liked to shop at the local stores. We just treated him like a regular guy, which is what he wanted. Later, we were getting beat up by the chain stores. One day, he called me up and said, "I'd like do a commercial for you." I said, "Andy, I can't afford to pay you." He said, "No, I want to do it for no charge." I said, "Andy, I can't let you do that." He said, "Well, I want do it. You've always helped me out with your store and I want to help you out."*

A few weeks later, Andy was at Seamark with a local crew that the Walters couple arranged for him. They did multiple takes, Andy often saying, "I didn't quite like that one."

Susie Walters said: "He really was a perfectionist. For a little one-minute commercial, it had to be perfect. We found out a lot about him about him and his craft. He was very much like Sheriff Andy Taylor. He appreciated a small town and a sense of community. He felt like he needed to give back. He believed in his community."

The commercial aired on local channels in the fall of 2001. "At about the same time, intentional or not, Food Lion began running a commercial using the famous whistling theme song from *The Andy Griffith Show*," the *Island Free Press* reported.

Andy, outraged, reportedly made an overseas phone call to a Food Lion executive and persuaded them to stop running the song.

Tim delivered groceries to Andy's house as he grew less mobile, sitting on his bed as Andy watched the AG show. "He'd tell me about the actors, how they really were in real life," Tim said.

In 2007, Andy invited the Walters couple to the local premiere of one of his comeback movies, *The Waitress*.

They eventually closed their local grocery store, in large part due to the Food Lion presence in their shopping center. But Andy had helped buy them a few more years.

Susie said: "We have very fond memories of him. I feel very honored to have known him. He really was an American icon. He was just a really good man. I think he had a good life, and Manteo is where his heart was."

One of Andy's local friends remembered: "Whether through his gift of oratory, his knack for making a memorable commercial, his anonymous financial support or simply his presence, Andy kept giving back."

Bruce MacDonald, a local bartender, remembered Andy showing up unannounced one Christmas Eve to read a Christmas story at Mount Olivet United Methodist Church in Manteo. Bruce had brought his mother and his two daughters. "It was so cool. He was twenty feet way, just reading a story to his Manteo people," Bruce said. "Something I'll never forget."

Danny Etheridge and his wife, Dina, served at the Wright Place for Youth in Manteo, a home for children and teenagers that were abused or neglected. Andy and Cindi gave support. Etheridge, as a child, had first encountered Andy at the Ben Franklin store in Manteo. "Andy came in, loud and barefoot, but I had never met him," Danny remembered. "My mom said, 'Go on and shake his hand. I did, and that is how I met Andy Griffith." Danny continued:

Many years later as I was mowing the lawn of the Wright Place, Andy stopped his car in the street and said, "Danny, I just saw your Mom the other day," and that is how Andy and Cindi introduced themselves to the Wright Place. The youth felt so privileged to know Andy. They loved to sit beside him in church singing hymns. Andy would come by the Youth Home during Open House and Christmastime. Andy gave each youth a $250 gift card for their Christmas. During the summer months, Andy and Cindi invited the staff and the Youth Home children to sit with him at The Lost Colony. *The youth felt so important to be sitting in Andy's personal reserved seats. A night the youth will never forget. Andy and Cindi made a difference in the life of one very special youth. This youth was invited to visit at the Griffiths' home. This youth sat beside them at church and ate with them at their home. Andy did not want praise, but rather to touch the lives of others.*

11

ANDY'S COMEBACKS

*A*s Andy stood up for his island and beach friends, he had waged his own fight to keep going in the work he loved. He loved comebacks. With his wife, Cindi, providing strong support, he was rolling. *Matlock* had been his first resurgence. Music was his second. Film would be his third.

He came back in music with gospel albums, singing and playing guitar. One of the albums, *I Love to Tell the Story*, released in 1996, won a Grammy for best country gospel album. Andy might have thought of the New Yorker who told him he'd never make it as a singer when he and Ainslie Pryor were in the Big Apple in 1952. The Grammy was Andy's first major recognition as an artist, never having won a Tony, Oscar or Emmy for his stage, film and TV work. "I never won anything before in my life, not even as an actor," Andy told reporters. He was laughing, his humor characteristically assuaging the hurt. The money, as always, helped, but best of all was the recognition.

In June 1998, Andy talked to me by phone from Roanoke Island for a column in my paper, the *Winston-Salem Journal*, about his latest gospel album, *Just As I Am*. He was gracious, patient and guarded.

Here is an abbreviated version of that column:

> *Andy Griffith believes that grace has been a mysterious and recurring factor in his life.*
>
> *"I keep thinking of the various turns in my life, that there's grace in there somewhere," he said last week.*
>
> *Griffith credits grace, or God's love, with the success of his 1996 country gospel album,* I Love to Tell the Story. *The album won a*

Grammy award for best country gospel album and has sold more than 2 million copies. He recently released a second gospel album on Sparrow Records, Just As I Am.

This is the man-next-door singing, a guy who has finally found happiness in his third marriage. He is a man who has been temperamental at times but has also established a $25,000 scholarship at the University of North Carolina for students in dramatic arts and music. He is a man, like many, who has been intrigued by grace since childhood.

In 1980 at his California home, he fell off a roof he had been repairing and broke his back. Grace pulled him through, he said. In the early '80s, he battled Guillain-Barre syndrome, a rare form of nerve inflammation. Grace—and his wife, Cindi—pulled him through.

Griffith has talked about faith when asked, but is not zealous about his religion. He has been quiet with his faith, much like his late friend Terry Sanford. Griffith campaigned over the years for Sanford, a former North Carolina governor and U.S. senator.

He said he does not agree with the Religious Right. "I just don't think that way." He doesn't buy all their definitions of sin, he said, but declined to elaborate. And so he has lived, a private man never far from grace.

He thinks about grace as he considers his new gospel career. At an age when many of his contemporaries are sagging in rocking chairs, Griffith has found success in an increasingly competitive field that first fascinated him more than half a century ago.

The surprises keep coming. In a package of fan mail Sparrow Records forwarded to him recently, he found a letter from Sanford complimentary of Griffith's new album. By the time Griffith read the words, his old friend was already dead.

Griffith was saddened by the fact that he would never be able to respond to his friend. But he was also happy to receive the letter, just a few kind words from another man with a quiet faith and fascination with grace.

Andy joked about the Grammy award to a good friend on the island, saying if he had known the music business had become so easy, he would have re-entered it years ago: if you hit a wrong vocal or guitar note, the producers just overdub it. But he was good on the records and proud of the award. It brought renewed interest to his music. Country superstar Brad Paisley sought out Andy. They became friends and sang together in a video for the song "Waitin' on a Woman," which was shot at the Tanger Outlet Mall in Nags Head. Paisley visited Andy at the island estate.

In the early 2000s, Andy hit his third comeback, taking supporting roles in three movies, *Daddy and Them*, with film outlaw Billy Bob Thornton; *The Waitress*; and *Play the Game*. Andy shone in each movie, delighting in the comedy, sometimes ribald. He and Thornton became close, Daniel de Vise writes in his book *Andy and Don*, sharing dinners at which Andy would get tight on wine and hug Thornton. Andy was taking chances, finding new ways to express himself through his art. He was determined to keep working, having once said, "retire and you start to die."

He agreed to do *Play the Game* for about $22,000, a fee that underscored how much he wanted to stay in movies and, perhaps, how much he wanted to support emerging artists.

Ron Howard told the author that he'd learned much about storytelling, creative integrity, authenticity and having a unique voice from Andy. "That really all stems from Andy," he said. Howard said he regretted not finding the right part for Andy in any of his movies. "I never had a good role for him. I once developed a script I hoped I would cast him in. I always dreamed of it, you know? I knew it had to be just right." If the part wasn't right, he said, the audience would be distracted by their reunion. When he was directing *The Da Vinci Code*, which came out in 2006, Howard said he consulted with Andy over a great dinner, learning from the story mechanics Andy had used in *Matlock*. "Andy had a real profound story sensitivity," Howard said.

As always, Andy drew strength from his island. In 2003, he talked to North Carolina journalist Jimmy Tomlin for a story in *Our State Magazine*. "This was a phone interview," my friend Jimmy told me, "and he happened to be talking to me from Hawaii. He was sitting on a hotel balcony overlooking the Pacific Ocean and he talked about how beautiful it was…pregnant pause… 'but I shore do miss home.' I was just really struck by that—he's in Hawaii, and he's homesick for Manteo."

12

ANDY'S BRIDGE TO THE FUTURE

For a man who doesn't want to be a politician, that was quite a speech....
Anytime the truth is out of style, we're all in a lot of trouble.
—Andy's character Professor Lewis Vernor,
in the 1978–79 TV miniseries Centennial

*I*n 2000, Andy lent his support to Mike Easley, the North Carolina attorney general and Democratic candidate for governor. Easley was running a tough race against Richard Vinroot, a Republican who was a former Charlotte mayor.

It was the latest step in his work in North Carolina politics, an effort that had started on the island.

Andy, close to *Lost Colony* icon Cora Mae Basnight, her daughters Della and Dotty Fry and the rest of her family, had watched Cora Mae's son Marc grow up. As Marc Basnight started in the state senate in the mid-1980s, Andy emceed a party for Basnight's fellow legislators at Basnight's island home, Andy's presence drawing a big bipartisan crowd and helping the newcomer rise to head of the state senate. Marc, like Andy, was a self-made man. Basnight's schooling was limited to his diploma from Manteo High School, but he was wicked smart in a disarming way and had made it in construction and, later, with a namesake restaurant. Speaking in his beautiful brogue, Basnight charmed and cajoled legislators far more formally educated than he was, eventually becoming more powerful than the governors of his time and bringing home millions for projects to better Dare County.

In 1989, some North Carolina Democratic leaders had tried to recruit Andy to run against incumbent Republican Jesse Helms for the U.S. Senate. Internal polls showed Andy could win the race, some said. In early June 1989, Andy, through Basnight, squelched the talk. Basnight said Andy, on the island, called him, saying, "I'm an actor. That's all I've ever known and all I've ever done." Basnight said Andy told him he "wasn't interested in running for anything and was surprised anyone would want him to."

Andy was wise to reject the push. He might well have won, and his very private self would have hated the very public job.

As Easley began his run for governor, an island buddy of Andy's suggested Easley recruit Andy to do a campaign commercial. One of Easley's media folks from up North asked him if he was sure that was a good idea, if people would remember Andy. Easley just shook his head and told the staffer to proceed with the commercial by all means. Easley was in awe of Andy and realized his widespread appeal, having grown up on a northeastern North Carolina tobacco farm watching the AG show.

In the summer of 2000, before making the commercial, Andy, on his island and being driven to see the woman who cut his hair, Donetta Livesay, had a heart attack that almost killed him.

The news did not break for several days, so Donetta wondered why the punctual Andy had missed his appointment. After attending to him every three weeks for years, she'd gotten to know him and his full head of hair. She'd watch *Matlock* when he was still doing the show and plane-commuting from the Wilmington set to Manteo, proud of her work. She cut his hair at her downtown shop at 8:00 a.m., careful to shield him, as much as possible, from fans. He was gracious to her and was the best of storytellers, telling her Don Knotts's role in the TV sitcom *Three's Company* diminished Don's acting skills and would affect his ability to get future acting roles. Don should be embarrassed, Andy said.

He also told her that David Janssen, one of his co-stars in the 1978–79 miniseries *Centennial*, was a drunk. "My take is that Janssen was extremely talented, and Andy wanted his potential to be reached," Donetta said. But usually, she said, Andy did not talk ill of others. "He was one smart man," Donetta said. "He was just delicious in every way."

Donetta charged Andy the same as her other patrons, about ten to twelve dollars a cut. Andy tipped her decently but not lavishly.

She learned he missed his appointment because of the heart attack, but the news was slow to surface because Andy was registered in a Norfolk hospital under another name. Andy told entertainment writer Mal Vincent of the *Virginian-Pilot* newspaper, one of the only reporters he'd ever opened up to, "I knew if they got wind of this in Hollywood, everybody would think I was dying and I'd never be insurable again."

Andy spent several days in the hospital. Once, he called out for his longtime island friend Dotty Fry. She paid him a visit.

Donetta complied with Cindi Griffith's request that she come to the hospital to cut Andy's hair. Donetta gingerly worked around the tubes running into his body. After he got back to the island, Andy wrote Donetta a July 25, 2000 letter of thanks in his neat cursive and simple letter-writing mode, far different from the wildly creative style that spilled from his big brain to assistants scribbling it down:

> *Dear Donetta,*
> *Thank you for caring so much that you came all the way to Norfolk to give me a hair cut* [sic]. *You are the best.*
> *I also appreciate you keeping me in your prayers.*
> *Andy*

Donetta treasures the letter.

That summer, Dare County sheriff Bert Austin and Sergeant Greg Wilson twice drove Andy to Chesapeake, Virginia, for doctor's appointments. Austin, driving, took a route that would ensure he'd be near hospitals on the way if Andy had a relapse and that there would be no traffic jams. On one of the trips, nurses met Andy with a guitar, Wilson said, hoping they would play him a song. Wilson, now a captain, found that unprofessional and bothersome. Another time, the lawmen told Andy they were going to eat lunch at Shoney's. Andy, who'd once done a commercial for the chain, told them Shoney's had fired him. Wilson said they'd eat elsewhere.

As they left the doctor's office on one trip, Andy told Wilson to drive, saying, "You drive back. The sheriff's too damn slow." Austin didn't have the heart to tell Andy that he'd driven slowly out of caution for his health.

As Andy recovered, he taped the commercial for Easley. It ran in the last weeks of the race and is often credited in helping Easley win. Pundits called it "The Mayberry Miracle."

"It was a great validation: This is a good North Carolina boy and you can trust him," said Gary Pearce, a North Carolina newspaper columnist and former top adviser to Governor Hunt. "Andy was just such a presence. He came from a hardscrabble background. He got a chance to attend Carolina, which changed his life. He saw how it lifted up people, the underdogs."

Andy spoke at Easley's inauguration, delivering the traditional "Tarheel toast," ending with the words, "The best land, the best land, the Old North State!"

When the applause finally subsided, Andy grinned and spoke his trademark words: "'ppreciate it." Easley soon followed, doing his best, but realizing Andy had "dropped the mic" on him.

In the years ahead, Andy and Easley drew close. They loved to joke with each other, "cuttin' the fool" as Easley called it. They had both started as underdogs. Easley had trouble reading in school and was sometimes called "lazy." He realized as an adult that he was dyslexic, finally understanding his early learning challenges. Easley said they were alike in that they both were engrossed when they were preparing for speeches, shunning personal contact in the time before. They were both charismatic, natural charmers, earthy storytellers who were, simultaneously and paradoxically, private people who excelled in public fields, using their talent and connections to rise. They shared a love of woodworking and music.

North Carolina governor Mike Easley and Andy play guitars in Andy's island home in the early 2000s. *Courtesy Mike Easley.*

The governor visited Andy on the island, playing guitars with him in Andy's original island house by a brick fireplace with Andy's awards on the mantel and, later, in the new house Andy and Cindi had built on their estate, patterned after Andy's Toluca Lake house in Los Angeles. The island, Easley said, was Andy's base. "It was where he found that one place he walked into and felt like the whole world had lifted off his shoulders."

Andy taught Easley's son Michael how to play "Whoa Mule" on Michael's banjo. Easley, his son and Andy would share Nabs, sodas and talk as they jammed. During one session, Easley thought he was doing well, taking off on his jamming. Andy looked up from his own strumming and wryly told Easley, "Maybe you better stick to being governor."

Andy, Easley said, counseled him on speeches, telling him about timing and how to resonate his voice. Andy agreed to do a commercial supporting Easley's push for education funding. Easley told Andy he might talk about how his parents pushed him to attend college. Andy gently corrected the governor: He could say they supported his efforts to attend, but they didn't take the initiative on the push. "He wouldn't say anything if it wasn't true," Easley said. "He was quite fastidious about that."

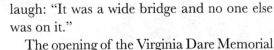

On August 16, 2002, Andy led in the opening of a new, four-lane bridge from mainland Dare County to Roanoke Island, driving his 1935 Packard convertible to the mainland with passengers Cindi; Easley and his wife, Mary; and Attorney General Roy Cooper, who would later become governor himself. Despite his love of cars, Andy was not a good driver, easily distracted by the scenes around him. But Easley remembered with a laugh: "It was a wide bridge and no one else was on it."

Andy at the bridge opening.
Drew C. Wilson photo.

The opening of the Virginia Dare Memorial Bridge was a milestone moment for Andy. When he first came from the Dare County mainland to the island, he'd arrived by ferry. Bridges had long since replaced the ferries. As the new $91 million bridge opened, Andy and Easley got out of Andy's car to an adoring crowd of four thousand on the island side. People rushed forward with cameras.

Andy at the wheel during the opening of the Virginia Dare Memorial Bridge. *Drew C. Wilson photo.*

Andy, Governor Mike Easley (*center*) and others at the bridge opening. *Photo by Drew C. Wilson.*

A woman gave her camera to Easley and asked him to take her picture with Andy, and more folks asked the same. The governor obliged them. He knew who the crowd was there to see.

Andy remained tight with Senator Basnight, including through their shared loved of Carolina basketball and their mutual friendship with the coach of the men's basketball team, Dean Smith. Smith shared their emphasis on fighting for underdogs and social justice, especially by improving public education. Andy was proud of having been a teacher, he once told Ron Howard.

When one of Smith's former assistant coaches, Roy Williams, accepted the head coach job in 2003, several years after Smith had retired, Basnight hosted Williams, Andy and Smith at his namesake restaurant on the Nags Head Causeway. Basnight's chief of staff, Rolf Blizzard, remembered: "I was fortunate enough to fly in with Coach Smith and Coach Williams. Even though Coach Williams was the new coach being introduced, the crowd flocked to Coach Smith. And when they met with Andy, I don't know who was more excited—Andy, Coach Smith or Coach Williams. A great day indeed."

Andy, who'd struggled to pay his tuition as a Carolina student, had long been among the Carolina elite. When he visited Chapel Hill for meetings, staying at the stately Carolina Inn, Julian's, the town's premier clothing shop—which designed clothes for Coach Williams and others—wheeled over racks of sports coats, shirts and pants. Andy would pick out what he wanted, and the staff would tailor the clothes for him, said Bart Fox, the custom clothing specialist for Julian's, which was established in 1942. Andy, he said, was humble, appreciative of the service.

Andy had been working out his ambivalent relationship with Mount Airy since October 2002, when he made his first public appearance in his hometown in more than forty years for the dedication of a section of U.S. Highway 52 as the Andy Griffith Parkway. Governor Easley was with him. Griffith, who had dismissed claims that Mayberry was based on Mount Airy, said that day, "People started saying Mayberry was based on Mount Airy," he said. "Sure sounds like, doesn't it?"

Andy and Governor Mike Easley at the dedication of the Andy Griffith Parkway in Mount Airy in 2002. *Photo by Sonny Hedgecock.*

The actor was clearly playing to his hometown crowd. His declaration in the 1990s that "Mount Airy is not Mayberry" and "If Mayberry is anywhere, it is Manteo" still stood, especially considering that he had built his life around Manteo. Andy never pulled back the Manteo statement, his strongest words about the Mayberry model.

Andy returned to Mount Airy in September 2004, when he attended a dedication of a statue of Sheriff Taylor and Opie walking with their fishing poles. The Surry Arts Council, under the leadership of executive director Tanya Jones, had worked hard to bring in Andy. Easley remembered the statue dedication as an emotional time for Andy.

Back on his island, Andy continued to stay active in political issues. One of his friends remembers:

In 2005, Roanoke Island's south end faced pressure from developers seeking to tie into Manteo's coveted central water and sewer system, the only municipal service of its kind on the entire Outer Banks. In a critical election, Andy once again breeched his island wall of anonymity, agreeing to appear at a campaign rally in the island community of Skyco in support of Manteo town commissioners up for reelection who opposed high-density development on an island with limited resources. Angel Ellis Khoury, who often collaborated as speechwriter on local topics with Andy and Cindi, worked with them on a campaign speech incorporating "What It Was, Was Football" to characterize the island's resources as something both sides—both pro- and anti-development—wanted. As the room was being readied for the evening rally on November 3, 2005, news came that Mayor Pro-Tem Dellerva "Del" Collins, one of the candidates Andy was hoping would win, had died of a heart attack. She was a beloved Black leader. After a brief discussion, all agreed that Del would want the rally to go on. To a packed house set back by the sad news, Andy delivered his familiar lines from his football monologue in service of a cause dear to his heart, protecting the island he loved. Townspeople re-elected Del to her seat posthumously, and then the Board

Above: Andy during his 2004 return
to Mount Airy for the dedication
of the statue of Sheriff Taylor and
Opie. *Photo by Sonny Hedgecock.*

Right: Andy at the statue dedication.
Photo by Sonny Hedgecock.

of Commissioners appointed her son, Darrell Collins, to fill her seat. The Manteo Board of Commissioners did not extend water and sewer to the south end of the island. And another cause championed by Andy won the day, even in the midst of tragedy.

Six days later after the November 3 rally, Andy was at the White House.

President George W. Bush had wanted to give Andy a Presidential Medal of Freedom. The Bush administration had called Andy, a die-hard Democrat, and given him the news. At first, Andy, seventy-nine, told one local friend he wasn't going to Washington to receive the honor from that "f——" Republican." Island friends encouraged Andy to take the honor.

He relented and went to the White House on November 9, 2005, wearing a dark three-piece pinstripe suit, an American flag on his left lapel. Andy smiled as Bush placed the medal around his neck, saying, "TV shows come and go, but there's only one Andy Griffith. And we thank him for being such a friendly and beloved presence in our American life." The president paraphrased Andy, saying the show "was about love. Barney would set himself up for a fall, and Andy would be there to catch him."

Dixie Griffith and Cindi Griffith smiled proudly near Andy.

Andy's fellow honorees included Muhammad Ali, Aretha Franklin and Andy's friend and fellow comedian Carol Burnett. He'd been on her show. When Andy returned to his island, he would sometimes privately don the presidential award for friends, clearly proud of it.

Andy sports his Presidential Medal of Freedom. *Courtesy John Wilson and William Parker.*

Several years later, Ron Howard asked Andy to do a commercial for President Barack Obama's Obamacare. Andy did so, telling Howard, "You know, we're celebrities, but we're citizens as well. When you find something you care about, you have got to risk that not everybody is going to like what you have to say."

Governor Easley and Andy loved to share laughs. During the 2009 inauguration for his successor, Bev Perdue, Easley, seated beside Andy, whispered to him that "I used to be a prince and now I am just a frog." Andy whispered back, "Reebick, Reebick."

Andy with Governor Mike Easley.
Drew C. Wilson photo.

"We were sitting in those aluminum chairs like you have at church picnics," Easley said, "and we both started laughing so hard. When Andy got to laughing, he always threw his hands up and leaned back. We leaned back onto the people behind us until they had to set our chairs straight!"

After leaving office, Easley faced legal trouble over campaign finance violations while he was in office. Andy called him, Easley said, asking, "You think they're going to try to get you in trouble?"

"I said, 'Andy, they can't. I didn't do anything wrong.'"

In November 2010, Easley entered a plea to one felony charge of failing to report a campaign flight. He paid a $1,000 fine. Andy never relented in his support for him. "A lot of people run and jump under rocks in something like that," Easley said. "Not Andy."

13

MELLOWING ON HIS ISLAND

I keep thinking of the various turns in my life,
that there's grace in there somewhere.
—Andy in a June 1998 interview with the author

*I*n the mid-1990s, Andy, approaching seventy, had puttered around the Roanoke Sound in his pontoon boat, pulling out from the wooden dock behind his estate, drinking from a tall plastic cup of white wine, "a traveler," taking it all in, loving the outlines of his pine-fringed, sand-beached island and the constantly changing colors and currents of his Sound, from tropical green, millpond calm to battleship gray, white-cap mean, the colors and currents mirroring his own moods from his first days on the island. The island, the one character he could never upstage. He would cruise by the back of the Waterside Theater, an old man in sunglasses lost in memories of his nascent days in the wild where it all started.

Out-of-town boaters who would have recognized him up close had no idea who he was from a distance. He liked it that way. They had no idea he'd played Sheriff Andy Taylor. They thought he was just some old man, a bit paunchy around the middle, with a Carolina Tar Heels lid on his silver hair.

They didn't know the journey he'd made, including the time he'd had filming *A Face in the Crowd* at the start of his career, sparking his lifelong friendship with one of his co-stars, Kentucky-born Pat Neal. They didn't know he'd struggled for years to land other serious dramatic roles and the things he'd done for money in the down times, ranging from that damn cracker commercial to the time in 1985 he was on TV's *Love Boat*, one of several co-stars that included that weird Andy Warhol. They didn't know he'd named one of his pontoon boats *The Honorable Jack Teagarden, King of the Trombone* in honor of a jazz trombonist and singer he'd grown up idolizing, one he once had on the AG show, playing a city councilman, another payback from Andy.

Locals passing him in boats knew him and waved. He returned the greetings. He continued to charm his fellow islanders.

Harrell Lee Bundy, an island legend in his own right who knows his way around the water and Shakespeare, was working on the bulkhead on Andy's property. He remembered Andy sauntering out in the afternoon, wearing only washed-out swimming trunks, a drink in one hand, to talk to him. Andy played dumb but was smart as hell, Bundy remembered. "He'd survived out there in Hollywood, never got too skinned-up," Bundy said.

Elizabeth Granitzki, a daughter of Andy's buddy "Doc" Harvey, said Andy "became, I think, more humble the older he got. I saw more smiles on his face when he was older."

When he found out Mary Carol Beeler shared a June 1 birthday, he took to calling her "my June girl."

"He had a way of just drawing you in with that beautiful smile and his Southern charm," she remembered. "Such a gentleman."

In the early 2000s, Andy drove around Manteo in his antique cars, stopping at ACE Hardware to get tools and supplies for his latest project. His father had been a skilled carpenter, and Andy never stopped thinking he could be one as well. Phil Brockway, the longtime caretaker of Andy's property, said he could always tell when he returned to work Monday if Andy if had been laboring on one of his carpentry projects: There'd be blood on the floor of the shop, and Andy might have a bandaged hand.

Phil, while not one to be starstruck, found Andy to be a fascinating, charismatic character with moods frequently shifting. "He was an actor," Phil remembered. "That's what he did for a living. If you're an actor, you can be anything you want, right? He was like nobody I'd ever met before. He had really old tastes in arts and furniture. He liked 1920s and 1930s furniture, like his cars, his generation."

Sometimes, one of Andy's antique cars would break down, and Phil would look up from his work to see a tow truck driving up, Andy in the passenger side and his vehicle of choice on a chain behind the truck.

But the cars usually worked. Andy often drove up the beach, stopping at the Austin Fish Co. in Nags Head on the Beach Road, the place started years ago by his drinking buddy Jimmy Austin, the wild and fun commercial fisherman. Andy would order flounder fillets and talk to Jimmy and his wife, Sandra; their daughter, Debbie; and his goddaughter Bea Bell, who ran the produce stand. Bea remembers Andy's eyes lighting up as they talked about her parents and other friends long departed. Andy had gotten handsome, she joked, once his face finally fleshed out, catching up with his big ears.

Andy and Cindi would eat at Nags Head at Owen's, Sam & Omie's and Penguin Isle, having, at Sam & Omie's, fried bluefish and coleslaw, and at Penguin Ise, sauteed soft-shell crabs with lemon and garlic. Several of the restaurants had a private space for him, "the Andy room," one where it was harder for tourists to bother him. Some waiters and waitresses adored him. Others found him grouchy.

The author Nancy Beach Gray remembered:

> *Andy ate at our restaurant, Queen Anne's Revenge in Wanchese, a few times. When he'd come in, the atmosphere in the dining room immediately changed as everyone zeroed in on him. Some fellow customers tried to act cool and give him his space and others unabashedly went up to his table and tried to chat. The waitstaff was always a little disappointed, finding him to be a bit surly.*

In general in public, Andy rebuffed overtures from tourists. In stores, he could be gruff in his resistance, autograph seekers not realizing that his arthritic hands didn't work as well as they once had and he couldn't sign if he didn't have his glasses, in addition to him just being tired. If people in a checkout line just mentioned store products or the weather and treated him like anyone else, he sometimes talked. But he did not want to answer questions about his work.

He was outspoken, even judgmental at times. When he saw Drew Wilson, a local photojournalist, smoking a cigarette, Andy lectured him, saying, "Only low-class people smoke." Ironic words coming from Andy, whose Sheriff Taylor occasionally smoked and who smoked heavily in real life until he quit. But Andy told Governor Easley that he regretted smoking on the

He also liked Steve

show because it set a bad example for young people. Smoking, Andy once said, had killed his father.

Another time, Drew came upon Andy in downtown Manteo unable to start one of his antique cars. Drew and two friends pushed the car down the street, with Andy behind the wheel, until the engine fired. Andy drove away without a word.

Others encountered a congenial Andy. One of Drew's co-workers at the *Virginian-Pilot* newspaper, reporter/columnist Paul South, remembers Andy asking him about his firstborn son, wanting to see a photo of him and gushing over it. Later, Andy saw Paul in the Manteo bookstore. Andy, headed to a birthday party for Elia Kazan, was looking for a gift for him.

John Harper, a local radio broadcaster and freelance journalist for the *Virginian Pilot*, remembers Andy being open and welcoming as he interviewed him about one of his gospel albums, especially when he realized Harper was well-versed in the musicians Andy had worked with and wanted to talk about the intricacies of making music and not show-biz gossip.

Andy liked to shop in downtown Manteo, stopping in at John "Possum" Silver's art gallery and buying some of Possum's fine paintings, including one of New Orleans's Preservation Hall Jazz Band.

He also liked Steve Brumfield's Manteo Booksellers, an island gathering spot for booklovers. Andy would take a seat in a wingback chair near the cash register and talk to Steve, whom he sometimes called "Steve-O," as he read a book or magazine. Andy sometimes talked about what a great friend Don Knotts was. Some patrons would recognize Andy, but Steve would give them a look that said, "Don't bother him." Andy mainly bought thriller novels but also bought some books on local history. "He was a sharp guy and always a really nice guy," Steve said.

Doug Doughtie, then a detective with the Dare County Sheriff's Office, remembered responding to a call at Andy's estate concerning someone who had cut down a cedar tree on Andy's property. Andy invited Doughtie, who was wearing a coat and a tie, and uniform Lieutenant Almey Gray to climb on his four-wheeler, a John Deere "Gator," so he could show them the damage, telling Gray to sit in the back "on the dog's seat" because "this boy [Doughtie] is dressed up pretty nice so we 'gone' let him sit on the good seat by me." Doughtie, who went on to become sheriff of Dare County, said Andy could not have been any nicer and eventually worked out things with the man who cut the tree down.

In the next few years, Andy's health began to decline. He had a bedrock support staff. There was Phil, the property caretaker, and Calvin Gibbs, his

Andy and his friend and construction man, Calvin Gibbs, on Andy's Gator. *Courtesy the Gibbs family.*

construction man and good friend, who built the new house for Andy and Cindi on their island property.

There was also Melissa Gibbs, Calvin's daughter, who functioned as Andy's "Girl Friday," performing unofficial nursing needs, always calling him "Mr. Andy," and Cheryl Hannant, who worked as his personal assistant, taking dictation for his letters, doing his online shopping, receiving his phone calls and processing his fan mail. The staff loved Andy and accepted his idiosyncrasies. He paid them decently but not lavishly, joking with them.

Andy often liked to hang out at his old house on his property, sitting at the kitchen counter and watching reruns of TV Westerns, including ones featuring Bob Armstrong, and the AG show. In a 1961 AG episode, Armstrong as an obstinate farmer stands tall and grim-faced with a pitchfork, going all American Gothic style over a bug-eyed Barney, surely a fun wink between Andy and Bob.

Andy would call out his lines before his character said them on the show. He had once said the shows were part of his life and he could not forget them. "They are something real to me, something that really happened," he said.

Andy's dogs Charlene Darling *(front)* and Jo Piney in the Sound. *Courtesy Melissa Gibbs.*

As he watched, he, he'd dip a butter knife into a jar of peanut butter and spread it on crackers, popping one into his mouth, then giving one to whichever of his yellow Labs was closest, be that Jo Piney, Charlene or the others. The crackers were not Ritz, Andy having long been done with the ribbing he got for doing the Ritz commercial when he needed the money.

Dixie Griffith, living in Colorado, kept up with her father through phone calls and a visit to his island home in April 2009. She sat by his bed and talked to him, reruns of *Batman* and *Bonanza* flickering on the big-screen TV, Jo Piney stretched out beside him. Andy was proud of Dixie and her children, his granddaughters Erin, Kimberly and Sara. Dixie would tell her father their latest accomplishments. His eyes would light up, and he would say, "Well, isn't that grand!" Sara, who attended Andy's alma mater, Carolina, made her own visit with Andy at his island home before she graduated in 2012.

Andy became increasingly focused on religion. He rejoined, from afar, his boyhood Moravian church in Mount Airy, often having the current minister, the Reverend Tony Hayworth, and his wife visit him at his island home. He also flirted with another denomination. Calvin Gibbs and his wife, Lori Ann, sometimes picked Andy up on Sunday mornings to take him to their Manns Harbor church, Harbor Light, which was Pentecostal. Followers of that brand of Christianity believe in the gifts of the spirit

Andy on one of his
last boat rides in the
Roanoke Sound.
*Courtesy John Wilson and
William Parker.*

of the New Testament: speaking in tongues, healing and prophecy, and are often lively in worship, in sharp contrast to Andy's sedate Moravian/ Methodist tradition.

On one visit to the Manns Harbor church, Lori Ann said, Andy excitedly raised his hands in the air along with other parishioners, grinning. "I think he felt the Holy Spirit for the first time," she said. "I knew what he was going through, because I had come from a faith tradition similar to Andy's," Lori Ann recalled. Calvin concurred and said Andy quit drinking because he didn't want his alcohol use to stop him from getting to heaven. Andy quietly bought the church a van.

Other friends of Andy say that he occasionally drank white wine, albeit sparingly, until shortly before he died. They say Andy did have a deep faith, starting off his mornings, sitting at his antique desk, with biblical readings guided by *The Upper Room*, a venerable Bible study guide.

In Andy's last years, Ron Howard told the author, he was "literally defeating some of those demons, some of that internal rage that Kazan recognized and tried to bring out in him."

Andy rode his Gator around the trails on his property, sometimes with a "traveler" of white wine in his cupholder. He was no longer able to take out his boat alone. Calvin and Lori Ann Gibbs took Andy out his boat, singing gospel songs at his request, including "Just a Closer Walk with Thee."

On Andy's eighty-fifth birthday, June 1, 2011, Melissa Gibbs and other friends took him out on his boat, Andy slowly sipping a glass of white wine.

14

ANDY'S "FINAL MARCH"

*T*here is a longstanding tradition at *The Lost Colony* near the start of each season, that of remembering alums who died in the previous year. Andy had long taken part in the ceremony at the Waterside Theater. These were his people, with whom he stayed involved, no matter what level of stardom they'd hit or had not, the ties that bound. In 2011, he slowly walked from a golf cart for the ceremony, standing apart from the crowd where he could be in the shade. "I had never seen him like that, and it was shocking and a little bit sad," Ira David Wood said. "I had the feeling it was the last time I would see him," said Wood, who would direct the pageant in the years ahead.

Andy was unable to make the last part of the ceremony, in which participants cast flowers on the Sound for the departed.

In 2012, Andy began to talk about what some Southerners call the "homecoming," the trip to heaven. He became bedridden, continuing to watch TV Westerns and the AG show. He wore nightshirts made for him by his favorite Chapel Hill clothing store, Julian's. When friends entered his room, he would pat the end of his bed and tell them to sit down and talk. He regretted not being able to save his son, Sam, he told Melissa Gibbs. He told her he'd sometimes been an "asshole" in his early years and regretted that.

On June 1, 2012, Andy's eighty-sixth birthday, some of his loved ones gathered around his bed. One of Calvin and Lori Ann's grandchildren, nine-month-old Adaylin, romped around, once falling on the remote control, causing the bed to vibrate. Lori Ann said. "Andy was laughing and carrying on, just happy to have a child in the room. It brought such joy to him," she said.

Andy loved to look out his first-floor bedside window across a pond to a hill Phil Brockway had landscaped, under Andy's close supervision. The hill was completely covered with flowers, ones that bloomed year-round. Skipper Bell would have been proud.

Andy was characteristically irreverent. At one point, he wanted to be cremated, his ashes scattered across his property, he told Phil, adding, "Just don't piss on my ashes." Later, he mandated that he be buried in a wooden coffin on his property. He wanted his burial to be done rapidly, saying he did not want it to start a traffic jam as those of other stars had done. His island friends did not need that, he said.

During 2012, Clare Dozier, a registered nurse, came by daily to see Andy. She went about her work professionally as she always had, not mentioning his star status. Finally, one day, Andy, with a sparkle in his eyes, told her, "You know I was in television? I had two TV shows."

Clare said she knew about that. Andy told her he liked playing Matlock more than Sheriff Taylor because the Matlock role was more challenging, and, apparently, because he did not like living up to the Sheriff Taylor role model. She remembers watching old Westerns with Andy, playing a game he started: Who could spot the future star? On one, *Wagon Train*, was Frances Bavier, "Aunt Bee." Andy told Clare that he and Bavier had "a disagreement" he did not define, but she called him late in her life and apologized, and he was proud of that.

He didn't like the criticism he'd received for standing up for President Obama, she said.

She remembered Andy driving his scooter around the house, shooing his beloved yellow Labs out of the way, saying. "Move girls!" She also remembered Andy reading his Bible daily and praying for forgiveness for any sins he might have committed.

As July 2012 began, Andy grew weaker. One night, Phil fixed Andy a favorite meal, grilled chicken breast, mashed-up red potatoes and asparagus, some of which Andy got down. Another night, Melissa fixed Andy another of his favorites, tomato soup with a cut-up hot dog in it.

On the night of July 2, Andy's friends drew close. Billy Parker talked with Andy about the beauty of the flowers by his window, spectacularly in bloom. Billy asked Andy if there was anything he could get him. Andy, who was having trouble breathing, joked, "Breath, Billy, breath."

As Calvin Gibbs bent down to hug Andy good-bye, Andy said, "Calvin, I love you, you'll never know how much!"

Calvin replied, "I love you too, I'll see you in the morning."

Andy said, "OK."

The sun is shining brilliantly, and all the earth is blossoming.
—Andy in a letter to his parents when he was in college at Chapel Hill

Early the next morning, July 3, Andy's doctor, Johnny Farrow, was called. Andy was getting progressively weaker. Dr. Farrow pronounced him dead at 7:00 a.m., writing on the death certificate that the immediate cause was "acute myocardial infarction," with coronary artery disease, hypertension and hyperlipidemia as related conditions.

Billy Parker heard minutes later. In his downtown Manteo yard, he gathered for Andy, that lover of gardening, pittosporum, long iris leaves, a piece of papyrus, orange cannas, orange lilies and red oleander. On the way to Andy's house, Billy culled a green hydrangea, some yellow lantana and sprig of pink roses, tying those together with the greenery and flowers from his yard.

Billy wrote in his notes of the day:

> *The small cadre of loved ones arriving at Andy's house could look down the long hall through open double doors to his bedroom. His body lay on the bed, his oldest yellow Lab, Jo Piney, pressed tight against it.*
>
> *Visitors ebbed and flowed between the entry hall and the kitchen, nibbling at fruit, eggs and banana bread. The conversation was subdued, but comfortable and easy, some of the old friends not having seen each other in a while.*

The funeral home staff placed Andy's body in a casket of brown wood. Then, and only then, did Jo Piney leave his side, going off to grieve by herself.

Andy's friends carried out his wishes for the quick burial on his property. Morning had broken. It was a fine one, the sun having risen over the nearby ocean a few hours before, the lead-in to another glorious day, maybe like the one Andy had seen when he first encountered the island sixty-five years before, touching the magic.

Billy wrote that he, Phil Brockway, Dr. Farrow, Calvin Gibbs and Calvin's son Kevin "rolled the coffin across the exposed-aggregate drive to the soft earth, brushing between the blue hydrangeas, to the grave site. It was under tall pines at the foot of a hill. Just around the corner was a spectacular massing of yellow and orange flowers."

Andy's people gathered around the casket. There was Cindi; Andy's longtime island friends Jack and Estelle Wilson; their son John and his partner, Billy; Phil Brockway; Cheryl Hannant; Calvin and Lori Ann Gibbs; Kevin Gibbs; Melissa Gibbs; Dr. Farrow and his wife; and a Methodist minister. The minister opened with a prayer and asked if anyone wanted to speak. Billy said he might read a poem. He noted that Emily Dickinson had written many poems about death, but that she'd written other kinds of poems, too, and that he wanted to read one that reminded him of "our many fortunate days here on Roanoke Island and the many sunrises and sunsets we've shared with people we love."

He read "I'll Tell You How the Sun Rose," including the lines:

I'll tell you how the sun rose
A ribbon at a time
The steeples swam in amethyst
The news like squirrels ran.
The hills untied their bonnets,
The bobolinks begun.
Then I said softly to myself,
"That must have been the sun!"

Lori Ann Gibbs then sang a hymn Cindi had asked her to perform. Lori Ann, in her sweet voice, broke into "Just a Closer Walk with Thee," which she and Andy had sung together recently when they were out in his boat, one of his favorites. It is a gospel standard Andy's Lonesome Rhodes belts out toward the end of *A Face in the Crowd*. The minister said another prayer, and the gathering held hands. Billy placed his flowers by the casket, joined by others with their own flowers. John Wilson said: "The ship was ready to sail, and he was aboard," tweaking a line Andy had once spoken on one of his surprise visits to the play.

The small group filed back to the house. The coffin was lowered, leaving a soft mound, carefully raked out, with the flowers atop, Billy wrote.

"Andy was the best friend I ever had," Calvin Gibbs would remember.

A few hours later, *The Lost Colony* announced on the internet that "Andy Griffith has taken his Final March," the last two words taken from the march of the vanishing colonists at the play's end and long used among the pageant family to announce the newly departed.

The news went worldwide. News copters circled Andy's estate, looking for funeral photos, but Andy's burial was done. He'd gone out quietly, just as he'd wanted, on the island that made him, leaving it in peace, setting the script until the end.

Flags across his island flew at half-mast. Near the guard gate to his property was a fan's tribute, a bouquet of orange day lilies with a card: "We'll miss you, Andy." In cottages and bars up the beach, Andy's fans raised toasts of good cheer to his passage, retelling stories of their encounters with the star who had graced them with his presence.

President Obama issued a statement: "Michelle and I were saddened to hear about the passing of Andy Griffith this morning. A performer of extraordinary talent, Andy was beloved by generations of fans and revered by entertainers who followed in his footsteps. He brought us characters from Sheriff Andy Taylor to Ben Matlock, and in the process, warmed the hearts of Americans everywhere. Our thoughts and prayers are with Andy's family."

The *New York Times* headlined his obituary with "TV's Lawman and Moral Compass."

Bob Armstrong died twenty-four days after Andy, at the age of ninety-five in California, leaving behind hundreds of roles in TV and movies. He and Andy had remained friends until the end, never forgetting their friend Ainslie Pryor, never forgetting their start on their isle of dreams, their magic compass.

EPILOGUE

Quentin Bell said Andy's small funeral should have been followed with a larger sendoff: "He did a lot for the state. And he did a lot for Dare County and for the island. Roanoke Island is where he really wanted to be."

Andy had come a long way from his foothills boyhood, working hard, rising high and fast, then courageously resetting himself to stay in the game with the art and resilience that his island had honed.

He left behind many gifts, including instructions for a nice house on the island for Melissa Gibbs and her daughter and son, a wish that Cindi Griffith carried out. Andy worried about Melissa as a single mom. The family, with a granddaughter, thrives today.

The Manteo High School band Andy restarted remains strong. "It worked out real good, because they couldn't kill that band now if they had to," Andy had joked in 1982. The band has positively affected countless students, including Ken Mann, who went on to become a popular local radio broadcaster and musician. "I wouldn't be who I am today if Andy had not started that band," said Mann, who played a deputy in "The Hunting Party."

The Outer Banks Community Foundation that Andy helped start continues to daily help hurting souls. As of February 2022, the assets of the foundation had reached over $25,000,000 to support grants and scholarships to benefit Outer Bankers, having steadily grown from its start of $90,000 in assets, and has given more than $11,000,000 in grants.

R.G. "Bob" Armstrong (*left*) playing the local sheriff during the filming of "The Hunting Party," with Ken Mann, playing a deputy. *Courtesy Ken Mann.*

Andy financially supported Outer Banks Conservationists, a nonprofit that preserves natural, cultural and historic resources, including Island Farm, which delights locals and visitors, just across U.S. 64 from Andy's property. Ron Howard donated $50,000 to the organization in memory of Andy, money that helped keep it going. Children helped by Andy's endorsement of broadband access are making their own way in the world, big ripples.

Food-A-Rama remains the island's local grocery, thanks to Andy helping lead the fight against Food Lion. Jackie Parker, the daughter of Andy's friend Chesley, runs the family store today. Proudly displayed in her office are framed photos of Andy at the 1978 opening.

Perhaps most important, Roanoke Island remains the most carefully developed area on the overdeveloped Outer Banks, thanks in large part to Andy's efforts. The Business U.S. 64 corridor leading into the North End from the old bridge to the mainland is free of billboards and laced with flowers, trees and a walkway as it runs past the entrance to the Waterside Theater and by the guard gate to Andy's property. Easy-walking downtown Manteo shines, a cosmic blend of a picturesque New England seafaring town and a tame Key West.

Andy made money with his art and through various ventures in other parts of the country but, quite intentionally, never ventured into development on the Outer Banks, though he could have easily grown his significant coffers by doing so.

Perhaps he did not live up to his early artistic promise. He was a child of the Great Depression worried about money who, after an astounding start on Broadway and Hollywood, went for the bucks with the AG show. It was damned good. Maybe he could have soared higher if he had left the show sooner and not been stereotyped as Sheriff Taylor. Perhaps he could have caught Hollywood stardom if he had not spent so much time stumping for Manteo revitalization and just becoming an islander in general. He left behind untapped potential of which we can only imagine. But *A Face in the Crowd* will stand for the ages and, more significant to most of Andy's fans, so will the AG show.

"You get a unique voice attached to the right format, that's where you make art," Ron Howard told the author in 2021. "*The Andy Griffith Show*, in its own very unpretentious, homespun way, is an American masterpiece. It's a work of art. There is nothing like it."

Andy in front of his Ford Bronco in the 1970s. *Courtesy Quentin Bell.*

Countless parents urge their children to watch the show's reruns, hoping they will absorb its lessons about caring for neighbors. Former governor Hunt, who watches the show daily, said his mere mention of Andy was an instant connection with people in his travels nationwide. "He was just one of the best North Carolinians who's ever been. And I know how much he loved his state and island." Andy's values, he said, "continue to impress on us the importance of helping others and doing the right thing. You see the goodness in treating people right."

Churches plan programs around those themes. Andy, who once planned to be a minister and resisted attempts to paint him as a role model, would 'ppreciate it. There had never been anything like Andy, and there never will be again.

He was a good man in all his complexities. He cared for his neighbors, repaying the spot of sand that took him in and made him. He was a good islander. Manteo was his real Mayberry.

ACKNOWLEDGEMENTS

*T*o begin to understand Andy, this ocean boy had to get out on Andy's Sound, the water he loved, with good guides. I am indebted to two island friends who took me out on their pretty boat one wonderful evening in August 2020, tracing the watery way Andy often took on his own vessel. On a fine spring day, when I had left my kayak behind, Quentin Bell, one of Andy's oldest friends, graciously lent me one of his kayaks to paddle Andy's home waters. Quentin also helped immensely with his memories of his long friendship with Andy and in sharing previously unpublished photos from their bond.

My late parents first turned me on to this story, telling me how Andy waltzed across their dreams when they watched him make his comedic breakthrough at the old Shrine Club in Nags Head in the early 1950s, a decade before I was born. Later, when I was a child, growing up at our family cottage in Nags Head, my family would catch glimpses of Andy barefoot around Manteo. He danced across my dreams and those of so many others. He was right there but still so magically far off for us children, this man we knew from the TV screen.

In college, I tried to age out of watching the AG show, but it was like cotton candy, the comforting stuff I could never leave, the whistled theme song echoing through the canyons of my mind. Later, I tried to fathom the man behind the actor, fueled by random sightings, sometimes with magic. One summer night in 1987, as my mother and I walked out of the venerable Owens Restaurant in Nags Head, we passed a silver-haired man walking in. My mother whispered to me: "That's Andy."

It hit me that she recognized him and I did not, that, almost forty years after seeing Andy make his comedic breakthrough less than a mile away, my mother, in her sixties, was remembering it all.

Dixie Griffith graciously shared with me memories of her father. Andy's widow, Cindi, cordially received my interview request but politely declined. My island buddy Claudia Fry Sluder Harrington, who grew up with Dixie and her brother, Sam, was invaluable in first helping me understand Andy as just another local, a high compliment from her, in his friendship with her family. Another friend, Susan Guthrie Lowrance, candidly shared with me her memories of dating Andy in the summer of 1972 and of later being married to his close friend from *The Lost Colony*, R.G. "Bob" Armstrong. My buddy Leon Rippy, a renowned character actor who got his start in *The Lost Colony*, years after Andy, helped me understand a North Carolinian making it in Hollywood.

My friend Drew C. Wilson generously shared many of the photos in this book. Two other photographer friends, Walter V. Gresham III and Sonny Hedgecock, shared key photos.

Samantha Crisp, Stuart Parks and Tama Creef of the Outer Banks History Center on the island, supported by state funds and local contributions, were, as always, an invaluable resource for documents and photos. The center, through the state archives, supplied numerous photos from the great Outer Banks shooter Aycock Brown, a friend of Andy's, part of a larger Aycock collection graciously given to the center by his family. The Roanoke Island Historical Association, through lebame houston (lowercase is her majestic style) provided two key photos.

My friend David Miller, a veteran *Lost Colony* hand who tirelessly carries on houston's work in preserving the history of the pageant with his own encyclopedic knowledge, always promptly answered my questions about Andy's time in the play and his support of it.

My friend and former colleague at the *Winston-Salem Journal*, Mick Scott, gave me access to the *Journal's* thick clip files on Andy. Newspaper friends Tim Clodfelter and Jimmy Tomlin gave me keen insight on Andy through their memories of interviewing him.

I am also indebted to these folks: Ron Howard, Donetta Livesay, Calvin and Lori Ann Gibbs, Melissa Gibbs, Gary Oliver, Craig Fincannon, former governors Mike Easley and Jim Hunt, Cheryl Hannant, Phil Brockway, Marjalene and Hunt Thomas, Quentin and June Bell, Ray and Linda White, Bea Bell, Sandra Austin, Thomas Daniels, Paul South, Liz Granitzki, Margaret Harvey, John Harper, Dare County Sheriff Doug Doughtie and former Sheriff Bert Austin, Captain Greg Wilson, Barbara Epperly, Ken Mann, Buddy Tillett, Gary Pearce, the late Edward Greene, Richard Lacerre, Susan Mayo, Liz Freeman, Aysha Apperson, Cate Kozack, Jeff Loy, McMullan Pruden, John "Possum" Silver, Harrell Lee Bundy, Connie Daniels, Claudia Jones, Johnnie Robbins Jr., Betsy Annese, Ira David Wood III, Jackie Parker, Dylan Swain, Steve Ausband, Carl Curnutte III, Susan Winstead, Kate Jenkins, Abigail Fleming, Jonny Foster, Ashley Randolph, John Wilson, William Parker, Greg Smrdel, former Manteo town manager James Ayers, Brian and Eddie Miller, Nettie Tisch, Cliff and Margo Blakely, Bruce MacDonald, Al Norman, Cam Choiniere, Bob Muller, Claire Dozier, Theresa Schneider, Louise Overman, Claudette Weston, Seth Effron, Bambie Smith Upton, Eric and Jack Sandberg and the late Della Basnight. Apologies to all I have unintentionally missed.

The Outer Banks Vintage Scrapbook on Facebook was a crucial resource. The hundreds of comments there on Andy, mostly from locals, helped immensely in contextualizing him and in giving me leads to sources.

As always, Sam & Omie's bar and restaurant in Nags Head, owned and run by my friend Carole Sykes, gave me a great place to meet key sources.

Thanks to my siblings, Richard, Jo and Mimi, who raised me up with Andy legends. The legacy of our turquoise cottage by the Nags Head sea lives. My daughter Molly, who hails from proud Outer Banks bloodlines, Midgetts and Griggs, keeps the stories coming.

I am indebted to two special island friends who first led me to the story of Andy's magic there and trusted me with it, opening the doors to all the others.

Most of all, thanks to my bride, Kathleen, for all the help in transforming my dreams into books. Into the mystic.

BIBLIOGRAPHY

$\mathcal{W}$ hile working on this book, I often felt like Andy, ever the wry and private man, was winking at me, knowing how challenging he had made my job. He thought out whole comedy routines in his head, rarely writing them down and leaving behind very few publicly written words of his own. A godsend came in the summer of 2020 when Samantha Crisp, the director of the Outer Banks History Center on Roanoke Island, shared with me an amazing, unpublished interview Andy did with his friend David Stick, a renowned Outer Banks historian, on Andy's love for the island. In that long interview, which can be read via the center, Andy sprinkles clues on the water.

I did hundreds of interviews with people who knew Andy, mostly fellow islanders, but also several of his friends and co-workers from afar. I also drew from an interview I did with him, as well as hundreds of stories in the *Winston-Salem Journal*, *Parade Magazine*, the *News & Observer of Raleigh*, the *Coastland Times*, the Associated Press, the *Virginian-Pilot* and the *New York Times* and records from the Manteo Board of Commissioners and the Dare County Register of Deeds.

These books were immensely helpful:

Collins, Terry. *The Andy Griffith Story: An Illustrated Biography*. Mount Airy, NC: Explorer Press, 1995.

de Visé, Daniel. *Andy & Don: The Making of a Friendship and a Classic American TV Show*. New York: Simon & Schuster, 2015.

Gray, R. Wayne, and Nancy Beach. *Legendary Locals of the Northern Outer Banks.* Charleston, SC: Arcadia Publishing, 2015.

———. Images of America: *Manteo.* Charleston, SC: Arcadia Publishing, 2020.

Howard, Ron, and Clint Howard. *The Boys.* New York: William Morrow, 2021.

Kelly, Richard. *The Andy Griffith Show.* Winston-Salem, NC: John F. Blair, 1981.

Khoury, Angel Ellis. *Manteo: A Roanoke Island Town.* Virginia Beach, VA: Donning Company/Publishers, 1999.

McAdoo, Carol, and Donald McAdoo. *Reflections of the Outer Banks.* Manteo, NC: Island Publishing House, 1976.

Schickel, Richard. *Elia Kazan: A Biography.* New York: HarperCollins Books, 2005.

Smrdel, Greg. *The Andy Griffith Show: Complete Trivia Guide.* CreateSpace Independent Publishing Platform. 2018.

Stick, David. *Aycock Brown's Outer Banks.* Virginia Beach, VA: Donning Company/Publishers, 1976.

ABOUT THE AUTHOR

*J*ohn Railey has spent much of his life on the Outer Banks. His previous book from The History Press, *The Lost Colony Murder on the Outer Banks: Seeking Justice for Brenda Joyce Holland* (2021), has been a top seller on the Banks. He is working on a screenplay based on Brenda's case. A graduate of the University of North Carolina at Chapel Hill, he is the former editorial page editor of the *Winston-Salem Journal*. He has contributed to the *Coastland Times* of the Banks and won numerous national, regional and state awards for his writing and investigative reporting. He is also the author of the memoir *Rage to Redemption in the Sterilization Age: A Confrontation with American Genocide.*

Visit us at
www.historypress.com